Business

Editor: Tracy Biram

Volume 381

independence
educational publishers

First published by Independence Educational Publishers

The Studio, High Green

Great Shelford

Cambridge CB22 5EG

England

ISBN-13: 978 1 86168 839 2

Printed in Great Britain

Zenith Print Group

Contents

Introduction

Business is Volume 381 in the **issues** series. The aim of the series is to offer current, diverse information about important issues in our world, from a UK perspective.

ABOUT BUSINESS

The landscape of business and trade in the UK is constantly changing. This book explores today's climate for businesses of all sizes. It looks at the challenges they face, successes, failures, and current statistics, particularly in relation to the double impact of Brexit and Covid-19. It also examines corporate responsibility; considering ethical business practice, diversity and inclusion and the huge problem of tax avoidance.

OUR SOURCES

Titles in the **issues** series are designed to function as educational resource books, providing a balanced overview of a specific subject.

The information in our books is comprised of facts, articles and opinions from many different sources, including:

♦ Newspaper reports and opinion pieces

♦ Website factsheets

♦ Magazine and journal articles

♦ Statistics and surveys

♦ Government reports

♦ Literature from special interest groups.

A NOTE ON CRITICAL EVALUATION

Because the information reprinted here is from a number of different sources, readers should bear in mind the origin of the text and whether the source is likely to have a particular bias when presenting information (or when conducting their research). It is hoped that, as you read about the many aspects of the issues explored in this book, you will critically evaluate the information presented.

It is important that you decide whether you are being presented with facts or opinions. Does the writer give a biased or unbiased report? If an opinion is being expressed, do you agree with the writer? Is there potential bias to the 'facts' or statistics behind an article?

ASSIGNMENTS

In the back of this book, you will find a selection of assignments designed to help you engage with the articles you have been reading and to explore your own opinions. Some tasks will take longer than others and there is a mixture of design, writing and research-based activities that you can complete alone or in a group.

FURTHER RESEARCH

At the end of each article we have listed its source and a website that you can visit if you would like to conduct your own research. Please remember to critically evaluate any sources that you consult and consider whether the information you are viewing is accurate and unbiased.

Useful Websites

www.companieshouse.blog.gov.uk

www.consultancy.uk

www.drapersonline.com

www.gov.uk

www.hjsrecovery.co.uk

www.independent.co.uk

www.ipsos.com

www.modernretail.co.uk

www.prospectmagazine.co.uk

www.simplybusiness.co.uk

www.shoutoutuk.org

www.telegraph.co.uk

www.transmitstartups.co.uk

www.theconversation.com

www.theguardian.com

www.yougov.co.uk

www.zerowastescotland.org.uk

What makes a good business idea?

By Suzy Jackson

There's nothing better than dreaming about starting a business. Apart from starting it, perhaps. But not all great business ideas turn out to be viable business opportunities.

So how do you assess if a new business idea has what it takes to flourish? Unfortunately there's no official 'ideas for small business' test. But asking if your small business idea stands up to the following questions is a good start.

1. Is there a market for my business idea?

Very thorough market research is an absolute must for new business ideas. If there's not enough demand for your product, your business will never take off.

Plus, it is really important to understand your customer before trying to sell to them. Writing a customer persona can help visualise and focus on your clients.

Don't forget, you are more likely to get your great business idea off the ground if it has a sound set of USPs - Unique Selling Points. This differentiates you from competitors and makes your product more desirable. Competitor research can help you understand the market better.

Things to remember:

♦ It is important to do thorough market research

♦ Understanding your market is key to success

♦ Competitor research helps you understand who you're up against

2. Does my business idea make life easier or solve a problem?

Every product serves a purpose - successful businesses are rarely built on novelty value. It could save people time, make a much-used process easier, or provide them with a new luxury. It's crucial to be clear about how your product

helps people, solves a specific problem or fills a gap in the market. Again, market research will help. If your business has an outstanding purpose that helps people then why not form a CIC - a community interest company?

Things to remember:

♦ Know what purpose your product serves

♦ Make sure this is in response to a market gap

♦ Market research

3. Is my business idea viable?

You need to be realistic. There's nothing wrong with being imaginative and brainstorming. But your business will only work if your product is technologically possible and manufacturing costs are feasible. You'll also need to think about the number of staff you'll need; whether you require premises...etc.

Unless you have lots of your own money to pour in, you need a business that can operate cheaply to begin with and doesn't require dozens of staff. Or you'll need to think about business finance and options for funding a new business. It is a good idea to write a business plan to help you think through the logistics of what you're considering.

Things to remember:

♦ Be realistic about what you can achieve with what you've got

♦ Low starting costs and fewer staff are more likely to work

♦ Business finance options can give you startup money, but you'll need a business plan

4. Can my business idea make money?

Work out how you'd make your product and how much you'd sell your product and/or service for. You need enough profit left over to sustain a business. Factor in employees' salaries, expenses, administration costs, labour, transport and material costs. The smaller your profit margin, the more demand you need to make up for it. Talk to manufacturers to find out about costs. Growing markets are going to appeal more to investors and provide better business opportunities.

Things to remember:

♦ Work out all costs

♦ Compare with the estimated sale price

♦ Smaller profit margin needs higher demand

5. Has my business idea got room for growth?

There are four main strategies to achieve business growth:

♦ market penetration

♦ product development

♦ market expansion

♦ diversification

Put simply, that means sell more to existing customers, start selling to new customers, or develop new products.

New technology provides enhanced opportunities to do this by automating processes and reaching people around the world.

It's best if plans for growth correspond with how the market you're working in looks set to develop over the next few years. Operating in an expanding sector is a much better guarantee for growth potential.

Avoid markets based on trends - you don't want your idea to become passé after a year or two.

Things to remember:

♦ Make a note of expanding sectors, more products and potential locations

♦ Look at how your market will develop

♦ Growth markets preferable

♦ Avoid trends

19 December 2019

How to start a business: a beginner's guide by an expert in strategy

An article from The Conversation.

THE CONVERSATION

By Lianne Taylor

2020 was the Chinese Year of the Rat – associated with the "rat-like qualities" of quick thinking and adaptability leading to success and wealth. After a year of challenges, with many people selecting or being forced into self-employment and starting a business, how can people mimic these qualities?

Online information meant to be helpful can instead be overwhelming. There are many predictions of where the future of business lies and how the post-pandemic world may create unexpected and surprising global trends towards growth and increased investment.

But when you are starting from scratch, you first need to understand the basics.

Who wants what I am selling?

The first step is figuring out who your target customer, user or audience is. Where do they shop and how will they perceive you? Data shows that online shopping in 2016 involved 1.66 billion digital buyers around the world – this has been forecast to grow to 2.14 billion by 2021.

The founder of Microsoft, Bill Gates, argues that selling is the one skill that entrepreneurs need. As your business grows, balancing sales with profit margins comes into sharp focus.

You can start your business in either structure, as a sole trader or limited company, without your offering being totally perfect. Build confidence incrementally, while testing the market with the "minimum viable product". In layman's terms, this means the most basic version of what you are offering that is saleable and works – and that a customer would want, without the bells and whistles that you can add later. It is normal to make changes after feedback.

Register your logo early. There are advantages, whether you are a limited company or not, such as avoiding anyone copying it. The British Library has free comprehensive resources to register trademarks and patents. It is worth checking your design for trademark infringement.

Starting as a sole trader means less scrutiny and regulatory compliance than a limited company – a more formal legal structure can follow. On the other hand, a limited company can make a better first impression to potential investors. Consider trademarks early on. You can register a limited company with dormant accounts just to secure the business name.

In both instances, insurance may be required to protect against public liabilities and product liabilities. If you employ staff, insurance is a legal requirement – and you will need to advise HMRC and pay PAYE. If, as a sole trader or limited company, you are using your car, you need to tell your insurer.

Business rates will apply to a room in your home used only as an office, but there are exempted buildings which you should check.

Whether you are a sole trader or a limited company, it's a good idea to register a website. Note that a limited company has more protection than a sole trader online. Social media domains also need to be considered. Free services that can help are the Federation of Small Business, the Institute of Directors and The Confederation of British Industry.

Will anyone buy my product or service?

Sole trading gives the impression that there is a person behind the brand, but limited companies can also tell a story and build trust with the customer, client or user. Question your potential customers, and use real data to understand the market. Market research will help you assess competition and risks – has someone already made what you are offering? What issues did they face?

An overlooked question is "why are you not using a product or service like mine?". Ask yourself and your target customers this. The answer will reveal whether what has stopped this service being created before is linked to anything from price, to accessibility.

Do not be discouraged with a negative answer. Try and come at it from a personal angle. Loyalty is key in building a strong customer base and telling people a story helps them to get to know you. Marketing – or in other words, letting people know you exist – in the digital age means you cannot avoid social media. Use microblogging sites if you are time poor or LinkedIn and paid-for reports, that give you insights into nationwide statistics on things like the cosmetics industry, market trends in your area of interest or information on social media use, although they can be pricey.

What's the plan?

Deciding whether to be a sole trader or a limited company inevitably means you produce a business plan. For both, it is a thought exercise, a useful checklist of decisions, justification, contingencies and research, predominantly for your own purposes, especially when it comes to being a sole trader. To allow for growth you might need to create another version for possible investors.

The business plan is not a linear document. Think ahead to future trends to recessionproof your business. Follow government policy on climate change through the Climate Change Committee – you don't want your product to be banned a year after you set up due to changing policy on plastics, for example.

Who should I speak to?

When building a network of people with experience and relevant knowledge, limited companies are regarded more seriously. Businesses need different types of networks – and the chances are that you already know several helpful people. Recommendations establish trust and can accelerate relationships. Mentors do not need to know you exist – you can read about successful business founders and learn from them without ever speaking to them.

2021 is the Year of the Ox, which signals hard work – but also recognition for that work. Choosing how to start your business ultimately lies with you doing your research and making an informed decision. Knowledge is power, after all.

9 December 2020

The future of ecommerce – 9 trends to watch out for in 2021

Ecommerce is developing quicker than Amazon can deliver, and that's saying something.

One minute we're marvelling at being able to order from the family computer and the next minute we're shouting at Alexa to re-order kitchen towel. The future of ecommerce is already here, and it's still changing.

To help you prepare your business for the next step in the ecommerce story, here are nine trends to watch out for in 2021:

1. Premium private label brands

Over the past few years, direct to consumer (D2C) commerce has exploded – giving brands direct access to customers and profits, and giving customers direct access to brands and lower prices.

But this trend is shifting.

If you associate D2C with cheap razor blades, affordable mattresses and trending makeup, then prepare to have your mind changed.

Premium private label brand sales are increasing, creating a new vertical in the D2C sector. Customers are turning to luxury private label brands for superior products and better shopping experiences.

2. Offline ecommerce

Let's take this blog offline for a minute. We all know that ecommerce is booming and rapidly catching up with traditional retail sales and depleting the high street.

However, there's a growing trend for taking ecommerce stores offline. Pop-up shops, interactive ecommerce kiosks, and bricks and mortar stores are all bringing our favourite online retailers onto the high street. Even Amazon is getting in on the action, with its chain of physical convenience stores.

In 2021, we will see an increase in ecommerce brands on the high street, occupying popup and multi-channel shops that bring the internet to real life.

3. Shoppable TV

We've all been there, watching the latest Netflix series and thinking "damn, that's a nice shirt." Well, soon enough you'll be able to click, find and purchase that damn good shirt.

Late last year, NBC rolled out shoppable TV ads that connect programs to a mobile phone app, enabling viewers to purchase what's on-screen. And it looks like this technology will soon be directly incorporated into smart televisions, giving a whole new worry to sitting on the remote.

Shoppable TV will finally connect viewing and shopping into a seamless experience that benefits both shoppers and retailers.

4. AI customer sourcing

Artificial intelligence is already used in ecommerce to make intelligent product recommendations, help customers visualise products better and assist you with customer queries. In 2021, AI is going to help find your customer for you too.

Intelligent algorithms will analyse current trends alongside your products, sales channels, customers and buyer behaviour to identify the best channels, time and price to list your products. This will save hours of number crunching, graph creating and report writing, and will help brands to accelerate sales and boost profits immediately.

5. ReCommerce

ReCommerce, also known as second-hand commerce, will see a renewed revival next year.

Recent research predicts the second-hand market to double within the next five years, but if you're thinking we've already been there and done that with eBay and Gumtree, think again.

With consumers becoming increasingly motivated by sustainability, rather than price, second-hand sales of luxury items will shake up the reCommerce industry. This presents an interesting opportunity for brands to open up their own reCommerce marketplace and turn second-hand shopping into an exciting shopping experience.

6. P2P and rentals

It's no secret that the ecommerce industry is grappling with a significant returns problem.

Dishonest customers are using returns windows to dress up for their latest Instagram story or satisfy their need for fast fashion, while honest consumers are returning items out of conscious consumerism. Could rentals be the solution?

Following the significant growth in P2P (peer-to-peer) platforms, many retailers are looking to expanding into rental ecommerce next year. By offering consumers the opportunity to rent clothing, furniture or electronics, you can increase audience reach while reducing returns.

7. Advanced customisation

Have you been on the Nike website recently? You can now customise every aspect of your Nike Airs, even the wording on the back.

Product customisation isn't new, but your ability to provide last-minute personalisation at an affordable cost is. 3D printing is changing manufacturing and fulfilment processes to enable quick customisations towards the end of the product journey.

Plus, with 3D printers becoming more affordable and available, it's only a matter of time before customisation becomes the norm.

8. Fulfilment

Of course, we couldn't write a blog on the future trends of ecommerce without touching upon the emerging tech in ecommerce logistics.

2021 will see increased use of autonomous deliveries, smart sensors, blockchain tracking, and digital twinning to increase delivery speeds, efficiencies and cost savings.

We could write a whole blog on the emerging trends in ecommerce logistics, so we did.

9. Smart home assistants

Alexa and Google Home have been great for turning on the lights, telling you the weather and playing your favourite radio stations. But they've also been quietly taking over the ecommerce industry.

Around 20% of smart speaker owners use them for shopping-related activities, whether that's ordering products, creating a reminder, conducting research or tracking deliveries.

This figure is expected to jump to 52% within the next four years.

If you're not currently optimising your ecommerce and fulfilment processes for voice search, get moving or get left behind.

How can you benefit?

If this year has told us anything, it's to always prepare for the unexpected. Whether you agree that these ecommerce trends will take off in 2021, or you think they've got a few years left, preparing your sales, marketing and fulfilment strategies for tomorrow's world of ecommerce will ensure your business isn't left behind.

19 June 2020

YouGov's Brexit and business study

Business decision makers say they are well-prepared for Brexit but believe the government has done a "poor job" of consulting and communicating on its plans.

By Connor Ibbetson – Data Journalist and Rudy Sooprayen – Director, B2B

Despite COVID-19 dominating headlines the Brexit transition period is nearing its end. A new YouGov Business Omnibus survey of 1,000 business decision makers in Great Britain explores how well businesses feel the government has consulted them, communicated progress, and also finds out how well prepared they are for what comes next.

Government consultation with businesses

While negotiations between the UK and EU about their future relationship continue, over half (54%) say the government has done either a somewhat (19%) or a very (35%) bad job on consulting business on the ongoing trade talks.

Among the various sectors, opinions vary. Retail businesses are split over the quality of the consultation with 45% saying the government consultation has been good and 43% saying it has been bad overall. This split sentiment is shared by IT and Telecoms businesses who are split 43% to 47% over whether the consultation has been good or bad as well.

Other sectors however have clearer opinions. Over half of hospitably and leisure businesses (57%) mark the government's consultation as bad, with 43% condemning it as "very bad". The legal profession is in agreement over the consultation, with an equal 57% of legal businesses saying the government has done a bad job.

Half of business people say the government has done a bad job of consulting businesses over the Brexit negotiations

Do you think the government has done a good or bad job of consulting business regarding the ongoing Brexit trade negotiations? (% of 1,000 business decision makers)

In total, **54%** of businesses say the government is doing a bad job of consulting businesses

A very good job	A somewhat good job	A somewhat bad job	A very bad job	Don't know
10	24	19	35	12

Government communication with businesses

Furthermore, two thirds of businesses (66%) think that the government's communication with them about its plans for a post-Brexit trade deal have been handled poorly, with 21% believing it has been "somewhat poor" and 45% saying it has been "very poor".

Only 28% regard the communication about the potential trade deal as being good, with construction (37%) and IT and Telecoms (36%) being the most likely to think this. At the other end of the scale, 20% of business leaders in hospitality and leisure feel the same.

Just one in twenty (5%) British businesses say they have had a high amount of communication about its plans for a post-Brexit trade agreement. One in six (17%) have had "some" and a quarter (25%) having had "not much" communication and approaching two in five (38%) say they have had "no communication at all". This is particularly the case among SMEs with half (50%) having not heard anything from the government compared to just a fifth (21%) of large businesses.

Six in ten business in the manufacturing (63%) and telecoms (60%) sectors have received at least some communication, with only

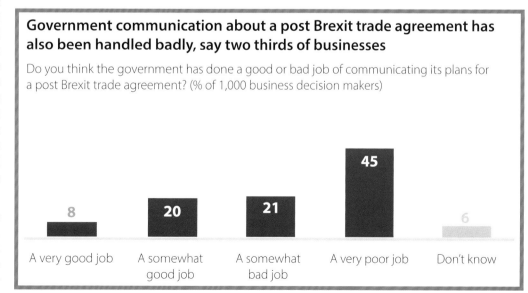

Government communication about a post Brexit trade agreement has also been handled badly, say two thirds of businesses

Do you think the government has done a good or bad job of communicating its plans for a post Brexit trade agreement? (% of 1,000 business decision makers)

A very good job	A somewhat good job	A somewhat bad job	A very poor job	Don't know
8	20	21	45	6

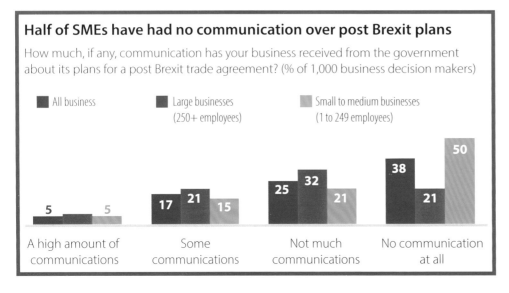

Half of SMEs have had no communication over post Brexit plans

How much, if any, communication has your business received from the government about its plans for a post Brexit trade agreement? (% of 1,000 business decision makers)

- All business
- Large businesses (250+ employees)
- Small to medium businesses (1 to 249 employees)

	A high amount of communications	Some communications	Not much communications	No communication at all
All business	5	17	25	38
Large businesses	5	21	32	21
Small to medium businesses	5	15	21	50

37% of those in hospitality saying the same.

There also appears to be regional differences with businesses. Those working primarily in London (54%) are more likely to have heard from government about its plans, compared to 47% working the Midlands, 45% in the East of England, and 43% in Scotland.

Most businesses are prepared for the end of the transition period

Despite many businesses feeling that the government has done a poor job consulting and communicating with them about what happens when the transition period ends, the majority of businesses (58%) do feel they are well set up for it. One in five (20%) are "very" well prepared for the change and nearing two in five (38%) are "somewhat" prepared. Meanwhile, 30% believe they are "somewhat" (19%) or "very" (11%) badly prepared.

Sectors such as manufacturing (71%), finance and accounting (66%) and those working in education (66%) are the most likely to report feeling prepared, while hospitality is the least likely sector to feel prepared (41%).

COVID-19 or no-deal Brexit: what would be the bigger business barrier in 2021?

2021 will see the continuing effect of the coronavirus pandemic on the economy and businesses may also have to handle a no-deal Brexit. But which do they see as the bigger barrier to growth next year? Half (52%) of businesses view COVID-19 as the greater barrier while 18% choose leaving the Brexit transition period without a trade deal.

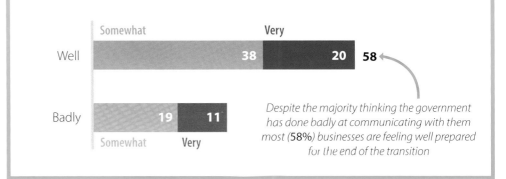

How well prepared are businesses for the end of the Brexit transition?

How well or poorly prepared do you think your company is for the end of the transition period (i.e. when the UK leaves the EU completely)? (% of 1,000 business decision makers)

	Somewhat	Very	
Well	38	20	58
Badly	19	11	
	Somewhat	Very	

Despite the majority thinking the government has done badly at communicating with them most (58%) businesses are feeling well prepared for the end of the transition

The threat of COVID as a barrier to business is acknowledged across the board by the most sectors, however some are more aware of a potential no-deal situation than others.

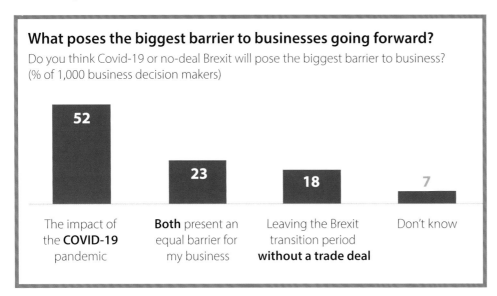

What poses the biggest barrier to businesses going forward?

Do you think Covid-19 or no-deal Brexit will pose the biggest barrier to business? (% of 1,000 business decision makers)

The impact of the **COVID-19** pandemic	**Both** present an equal barrier for my business	Leaving the Brexit transition period **without a trade deal**	Don't know
52	23	18	7

Businesses in the Retail (25%) and IT and Telecoms (24%) sectors are most likely to report that a no-deal scenario would be their biggest barrier, compared to just 10% of the hospitality and leisure sector who are the least likely to think that leaving the EU without a trade deal would pose a bigger barrier than COVID-19.

21 October 2020

Two-thirds of Captains of Industry believe the economy will get worse over the next 12 months

In the latest Captains of Industry survey by Ipsos MORI, 66% of Britain's business elite say they believe the country's economy will get worse over the next 12 months.

By Kelly Beaver, Managing Director, Public Affairs

♦ **9 in 10 agree the impact of COVID-19 is one of the most important issues facing Britain today**

♦ **Two-thirds (66%) agree that the Government's policies will improve the state of the British economy**

♦ **Two-thirds say the way the Government handles Britain's transition out of the EU is important to their business**

♦ **A third see no opportunities for their company in relation to Brexit**

Economy and business challenges

In the latest Captains of Industry survey by Ipsos MORI, 66% of Britain's business elite say they believe the country's economy will get worse over the next 12 months. Only 30% expect it to improve while 4% say it will stay the same.

In the survey, which spoke to over 100 Captains of Industry, widely acknowledged as the authoritative source of opinion on Britain's business elite, almost 9 in 10 (86%) of these Captains see the impact of COVID-19 as one of the most important issues facing Britain today. While around half see Brexit and economic uncertainty as the single most important issue (52% and 49% respectively).

While general expectations appear to be negative, Captains are more enthusiastic when it comes to their own companies. Over 60% believe business for their company will improve or stay the same (42% and 21% respectively) while a third (35%) say it will get worse over the next 12 months.

When it comes to these companies, their Captains are more concerned with economic uncertainty (59%) than they are with the impact of coronavirus (49%). A quarter see maintaining and retaining staff as one of the most important problems facing their company and only 16% see Brexit uncertainty as a significant obstacle.

Two-thirds (66%) agree that the Government's policies will improve the state of the British economy, including 14% who strongly agree, while only 1 in 5 (21%) disagree.

Looking to future action, more than 4 in 5 (82%) Captains want the Government to focus investment on regions such as the North of England in order to grow those areas and reduce regional inequalities, with only 8% disagreeing. Meanwhile, only 18% agree that the Government should focus investment on London and its surrounding area, 62% disagree. Over half (54%) believe the Government's industrial strategy will encourage economic growth in this country.

Two thirds of Captains expect the economic condition of the country to worsen over the next 12 months

C.1 Do you think that the general economic condition of the country will improve, stay the same or get worse over the next 12 months?

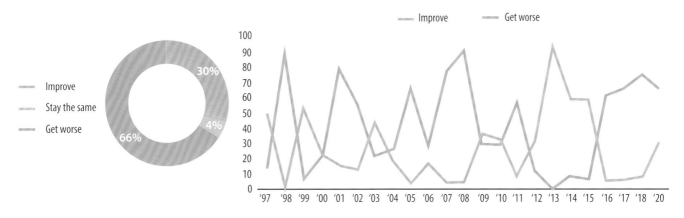

Base: British Captains of Industry (102) Feb - July 2020

Two thirds (66%) show confidence that the government's economic policy will improve the state of the economy in the long term

C.3 To what extent do you agree with the following statement? In the long term, this Government's policies will improve the state of the British economy

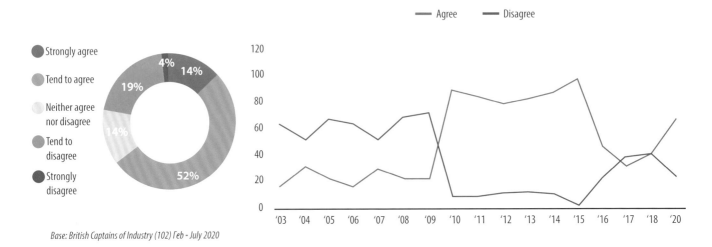

Base: British Captains of Industry (102) Feb - July 2020

There is strong support that regional inequalities should be reduced

C3. To what extent do you agree or disagree with the following statements (%).

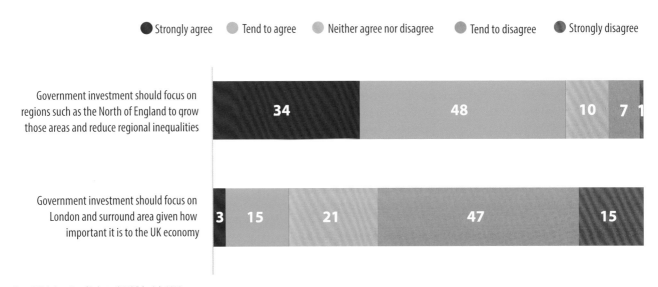

Base: British Captains of Industry (102) Feb - July 2020

Impact of COVID-19

Almost all Captains say coronavirus poses a moderate to very high threat to the UK economy (98%), including 56% who say it poses a very high threat. Nine in ten (91%) believe it poses a threat to the world.

Four in ten (82%) are concerned about the risk posed to their business and their workforce, while 83% are worried about the effect on their supply chain. Seventy-eight per cent say COVID-19 poses a moderate to very high threat to their costs while 37% say the same about their exports. While half (54%) say there is only low to very low threat of coronavirus affecting their R&D.

Forty-four per cent of those asked said they have used or plan to use the coronavirus job retention scheme while 38% say they have/ plan to defer their VAT payment. One in five (18%) have provided/ plan to provide statutory sick pay for those advised to self-isolate and 4% have/ plan to use the Coronavirus Large Business Interruption Loan Scheme. A quarter (24%) are not planning to use any Government support activities during the pandemic.

Almost 6 in 10 Captains (58%) say the Government have handled the coronavirus well so far, with 42% believing that they have handled it badly, including 13% who say very badly.

More than 8 out of 10 Captains think that coronavirus represents a very high/high threat to the UK economy

SR14. What level of threat do you think coronavirus poses to each of the following? (1%)

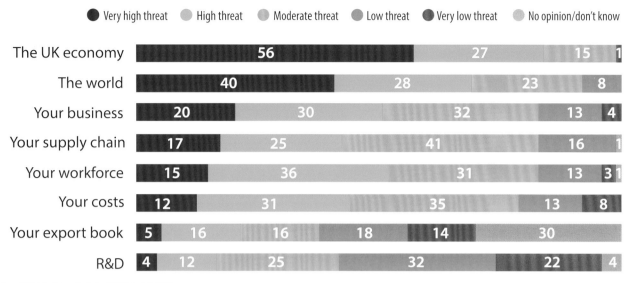

● Very high threat   ○ High threat   ○ Moderate threat   ○ Low threat   ● Very low threat   ○ No opinion/don't know

	Very high	High	Moderate	Low	Very low	No opinion
The UK economy	56	27		15		1
The world	40	28		23	8	
Your business	20	30	32		13	4
Your supply chain	17	25	41		16	1
Your workforce	15	36	31		13	3, 1
Your costs	12	31	35		13	8
Your export book	5	16	16	18	14	30
R&D	4	12	25	32		22	4

Base: British Captains of Industry (102) Feb - July 2020

Impact of Brexit

Two-thirds of Captains (66%) agree that how well the Government handles the Brexit transition period is important to their business, including 40% who strongly agree. Only 31% disagree.

Free movement of goods/ frictionless trading/ access to custom union is considered the most important thing for the UK to obtain in negotiations with the EU, half (47%) of

Captains see this is important. A further 2 in 5 (40%) want to see freedom of movement/ access to skilled labour/ clarity on EU national employees.

Over a third (35%) of Captains see no opportunities for their company in relation to Brexit. However, some see opportunities in the new markets beyond the EU (14%), increased inward investment (7%) and an opened access to skilled workers from outside of the EU (7%), among others.

Captains who trade internationally perceive mixed opportunities in relation to Brexit for their company, with a fifth (21%) anticipating new market opportunities beyond the EU

CEU21. What opportunities do you see in relation to Brexit for your company?

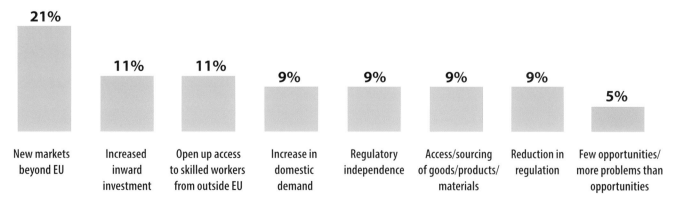

New markets beyond EU	Increased inward investment	Open up access to skilled workers from outside EU	Increase in domestic demand	Regulatory independence	Access/sourcing of goods/products/ materials	Reduction in regulation	Few opportunities/ more problems than opportunities
21%	11%	11%	9%	9%	9%	9%	5%

Top mentions

Half of the Captains of Industry surveyed (51%) expect that barriers to trade and tariffs for their products and services will get worse as a result of leaving the UK, while 11% expect them to get better and a third (34%) say they will stay the same. Two-thirds expect the ability to recruit skilled staff to get harder (65%) while 42% expect the ability to retain skilled staff to get worse.

Three in five (62%) expect to see free trade negotiations with major non-EU countries getbetter, however opinion is split as to whether there will be increasing investment in Britain; 43% believe it will get better while 48% expect it to get worse.

Only a quarter of Captains (24%) are optimistic that the UK will be able to quickly sign beneficial trade deals with major powers, while two-thirds (67%) feel pessimistic, including a quarter (25%) who feel very pessimistic. Similarly, 68% do not think that such deals will compensate for any loss of trade with the EU for the UK as a whole, 30% believe they will help.

When looking to the outcome of the Brexit transition period, half (52%) of the Captains of Industry expect a UK-EU trade deal to come into place, covering some but not all sectors. A further 35% expect to see the transition period extended while 12% believe the UK will exit the transition period without a trade deal.

Kelly Beaver - Managing Director of Public Affairs, Ipsos MORI said:

"The insight into the hopes and concerns of British businesses on the economy is incredibly important to understanding where businesses believe the economy is headed. The immediate concerns of COVID-19 are dominating but it's clear that there continue to be longer term concerns about Brexit and its impact on the economy and business. But the significant uptick in belief amongst business leaders that the Government's economic policy will improve the state of the economy in the long term will be greeted with relief by Rishi Sunak."

Technical Note

Ipsos MORI conducted 102 interviews with participants from the top 500 companies by turnover and the top 100 by capital employed in the UK. Participants were Chairmen, Chief Executive Officers, Managing Directors/ Chief Operating Officers, Financial Directors or other executive board directors. Interviews were primarily carried out by telephone/video conferencing due to COVID-19 (9 were conducted face to face before lockdown). Fieldwork took place between February and July 2020.

1 September 2020

Majority of Captains expect the government's focus on industrial policy relevant to Britain to improve as a result of leaving the EU, however, they expect the ability to recruit skilled staff to worsen

EU10. Do you expect each of the following to get better or worse as a result of the UK leaving the EU?

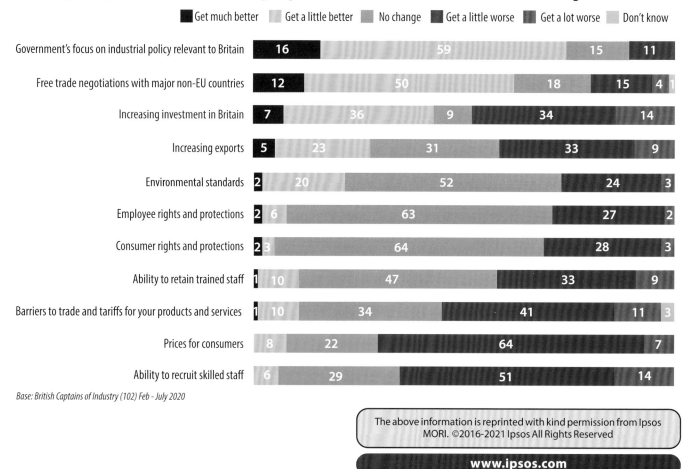

Base: British Captains of Industry (102) Feb - July 2020

UK firms fear twin force of Covid plus Brexit will force them under

More than 250,000 small businesses expect to fail in 2021 as state support 'dwindles'.

By Rob Davies

Small businesses and manufacturers are bracing themselves for a fight for survival this year, according to fresh survey data, as they negotiate the twin threats of Covid-19 and weaker post-Brexit trade with the EU.

More than 250,000 small firms expect to fold without further government financial support, according to a quarterly poll by the Federation of Small Businesses (FSB).

Manufacturers' trade body Make UK said its members expected lower investment in the UK and to have a harder time recruiting talent.

Just under 5% of the 1,400 companies surveyed by the FSB said they were expecting to close down this year, the largest proportion in the history of the trade body's Small Business Index, established in the wake of the 2008 banking crash.

If the same degree of pessimism applies across the UK's 5.9m small businesses, that would suggest as many as 295,000 fear they will go under.

The vast majority of firms surveyed, 80%, did not expect their prospects to improve over the next three months, with tough lockdown restrictions likely to stay in place.

Close to a quarter had cut staff over the last three months, while one in seven expected to do so between now and the end of March, raising a question mark over the futures of 16.8 million people who work for small businesses.

The FSB's national chair, Mike Cherry, said the amount of government support available had dwindled as the pandemic raged on.

"At the outset of the first national lockdown, the UK government was bold," he said. "The support mechanisms put in place weren't perfect, but they were an exceptionally good starting point. That's why it's so disappointing that it's met this lockdown with a whimper."

He welcomed support for retail, leisure and hospitality businesses but said that many were "still being left out in the cold", including company directors, the newly self-employed, supply chains and firms without commercial premises.

The FSB published a five-point plan to assist small businesses, including grants, income support and extended debt relief.

But it warned that firms already lacked the cash to cope with the tough trading environment, particularly given the costs associated with adjusting to the UK's new trading relationship with the EU.

Almost half of the FSB's members expect international sales to fall, up from 33% last year.

And survey data from Make UK, in partnership with accounting firm PwC, indicates that its members feel the same way about the post-Brexit challenge.

A third of companies said they expected investment prospects for UK businesses to decrease following the departure from the EU, with just 18% of companies believing they will improve.

Just over a quarter believed exports to the EU would fall with just 16% believing they would increase, while a third believed the UK's ability to attract international talent would fall.

Customs delays, cited by 47% of firms, are seen as the biggest risk to companies while concerns over national and local lockdowns were the second biggest risk at 46%.

Make UK's chief executive, Stephen Phipson, said: "The transition to new trading arrangements with the EU was always going to be the biggest challenge facing manufacturers this year and the fact we have an agreement in place doesn't alter that."

He called for a bold industrial strategy that goes beyond "short-term tinkering", instead laying out a plan for the next decade.

As firms voiced their concern about the future, an index tracking business output fell to its lowest ever level, below even the post-banking crash recession.

The BDO Output Index, which measures economic data from the UK's main business surveys, averaged 73.62 in 2020, well below the previous low of 83.28, recorded in 2009.

"These figures reinforce just how stark the economic impact of the pandemic has been," said BDO partner Kaley Crossthwaite.

"As we enter a third national lockdown, crippling challenges will continue to plague businesses in the weeks and months ahead.

"Successful and rapid rollout of Covid-19 vaccines will be the single biggest driver of business recovery."

11 January 2021

Shapeshifting to survive: Lockdown business success stories

We may be under lockdown but human ingenuity is not out the window. Quite the opposite, in fact.

By Victoria Miller

The current coronavirus pandemic has been sending shock waves across the globe. We are not only being confronted with the incalculable human loss, but we are also being presented with the sobering economic cost.

Not a day goes by without the media covering some form of economic news, current and forecasted, painting a gloomy picture. From alarming Bank of England reports stating that we could face the worst economic slump in 300 years to a ONS survey conducted in April showing that nearly 60 per cent of businesses have suffered falls in sales since mid-March. Businesses, large and small, are by no means immune to the virus' effects.

But with small businesses' greater sensitivity to market changes, what of their much-needed survival? They contribute hugely to job creation in the UK and account for 60 per cent of all private-sector employment. Many colourfully decorate our high streets and, unlike their corporate cousins, we see the faces and meet the characters behind them.

Efforts to contain the virus have led to the closing of bricks and mortar and to see them struggle feels personal to the communities in which they serve.

Observing optimism

Though small businesses are struggling, there is still room for optimism. Looking around my local area of Kennington and its various independent shops and restaurants, I have witnessed differing responses to the lockdown. Two favoured restaurants have taken different approaches: one has turned itself into a take away, while the other has deftly transformed itself into a quasi-farmers' market. My local bakery shut up shop but continues to do a good trade from the kitchen at the back. Then there is a local florist who 'put a notice in the window' for customers to email her for orders. I contacted all four businesses requesting to speak to them about their experiences. Only the florist was open to interview — perhaps a mark of the heightened sensitivities people are feeling at this present time.

Flower power

Speaking to Mary Woolcot, owner of Windmill Flowers, positioned in the quaintly named Windmill Row, it became clear that this pandemic has pushed her to focus on customer retention and growth more than ever. Despite trading in Kennington for almost ten years and having built up a loyal local customer base, the pandemic has resulted in 'a big slump in income' and seen her apply for government business support. This 'provides comfort in knowing that that the rent will be paid' but it cannot be the long-term coping strategy.

Unlike other fellow florists who supply hotels and restaurants, Mary's business focuses on individual custom which, in some ways, has afforded her some protection. 'Demand is still there' she is keen to tell me but this, she has realised, is not enough to keep competition at bay. A 'bone of contention' has come from stores such as Tesco who remain open due to their 'essential' status and thus, can continue to sell flowers. This, she declares, 'has made me realise that I need to be more aggressive with my website … I need a stronger online presence'. The last few weeks has seen her speaking to web designers to 'generate more online orders'.

But the pandemic has also brought to the fore a key distinguishing feature: bespoke floral service. Flower buying is a sensory experience, I point out, so how can she still deliver a bespoke service online? 'I always follow up with a phone call to find out if the bouquet is for anything in particular'. Will that not be more labour-intensive when business picks up? I ask. She doesn't think so, hoping that her enhanced online presence will lead to more orders, and the hiring of more people to help out.

She also contests her 'non-essential' status. She has seen a surge in funeral flower orders, crucial at such sorrowful occasions. In this sense, she views her business as serving a more meaningful purpose than purely decorative.

Mary is also giving her business thought for when we enter a 'new normal'. Hitherto, many orders have been through floral delivery companies which take 20 per cent of the cut. But by increasing her online presence, she poses assertively, 'why can't I do [that] on my own with my own website?' I sense the pandemic has given Mary greater business clarity. It has forced her to hone in on an underexploited area. Her new-found confidence will hopefully see her through this trying time, giving her business a greater chance to flourish.

Flour power

It isn't only current business owners who are adapting during the crisis. It may seem a wild idea to set up a business given such circumstances, but that is just what Pippa Morris has done with her new business: Balham Bakes. Her 'dream of having a bakery' for a long time seemed to be just that, but with the extra time on her hands she has been able to revisit this dream. With all local bakeries closing, Pippa saw it as 'a good opportunity to try out my idea on a small scale' and serve the local community with homemade baked goods. Aside from the sugar high — a definite feel-good factor — a percentage of her profits goes to the NHS.

Instagram, initially, helped her to grow her customer base but it was an encounter with Balham Newsie that saw Pippa's followers 'more than double overnight'. For all the marketing wonders that Instagram offers fledging businesses, it only

goes so far. 'A lot of people ask me if I have a website to look at … they don't fully trust Instagram'. The initial sales she received through Instagram however are being reinvested in the business, with a focus on building a website and marketing.

It isn't just marketing and web design skills which she has procured. Seeing her business come to life from concept to creation through to customer sales has taught her much about the small business strategy. Especially, when it comes to balancing her books, something that has been a particular challenge as her key ingredient, flour, has been in high demand. Excel has provided her with a means to track orders and income, enabling Pippa to 'become an Excel wizard'. Alongside Excel, she has developed 'a whole new range of IT skills that I didn't know existed at all'. These newfound skills she has transferred to her day job which, she states, she feels very fortunate to still have.

To start a business is always an uphill battle but in an already difficult financial climate, what have been her key challenges? Pippa ruminates. Aside from obtaining flour, working around her current job and increasing Balham Bakes' profile (so no biggies there then), the real challenge, she asserts, will come post-pandemic. It isn't just the loss of ease which she currently has to work around her job, but also the competition of other bakeries reopening that will prove the hardest. She is already planning ahead to counter this.

When the lockdown eases, people will want to gather with family and friends and she 'hopes to adapt into that market and cater' for these celebrations by offering a range of desserts.

Pippa's dream of owning a bakery could very well become a reality. She hopes that it will be 'the start of another career opportunity'. If she goes from city worker to baker, that would be the ultimate in shapeshifting success stories during this pandemic.

Survival of the most adaptable

Speaking to both Mary and Pippa, I sense that this pandemic has spurred them on to realise new heights for their businesses and dreams. While they are only two examples, they demonstrate that with forethought, confidence and determination, businesses, new and established, can adapt to the challenges faced, affirming that oft-hailed agility and dynamism. This flexibility allows them to serve communities more immediately where larger corporations have failed.

Small businesses are vital components of a healthy economic ecosystem and they will no doubt be at the heart of its economic recovery. While writing this article, I couldn't help but be reminded of Charles Darwin's widely quoted phrase:

'It is not the strongest of the species that survives … It is the one that is most adaptable to change'.

And for small businesses facing such testing economic times, this has never rung more true. It really will be survival of the most adaptable.

12 May 2020

Crowdfunding: is it right for your small business?

By Jessie Day

Crowdfunding is a game-changer for thousands of small businesses. But how does it work and where should you go to get started? Crucially, do you pay back crowdfunding once you're rolling?

According to Yahoo Finance, the global crowdfunding market is set to grow at a rate of 16 per cent over the next five years. Social media has played a big part, providing immediate, clear marketing campaigns and ready-made platforms for businesses looking to mobilise engaged audiences, raising cash while avoiding the bank.

Here's how it works, and how you can get started.

What is crowdfunding?

Crowdfunding is a strategy for raising finance. You ask lots of people at once for small individual amounts of money, usually through an online platform. You'll need to decide on a target figure, pitch the details of your next business phase or project to your would-be 'crowd' of investors, and then raise the full amount to go ahead.

Are there different types?

Yes, and it's important to remember that some forms of crowdfunding – for example reward and donation-based crowdfunding – aren't regulated by the Financial Conduct Authority (FCA).

Here are some of the different types you can use:

- ◆ investment-based crowdfunding – people invest in your business for a stake in return

- ◆ loan-based crowdfunding – money is lent to your business at a set interest rate, also known as peer-to-peer or peer-to-business lending

- ◆ reward-based crowdfunding – you give a reward in return for someone's investment, usually linked to the project you're promoting

- ◆ donation-based crowdfunding – people donate to your charity or cause, sometimes for something promised in return

How does crowdfunding work?

You'll usually use an online crowdfunding website to register your project and start raising money. We've listed a few of the most popular sites below.

Getting started (and the best crowdfunding sites for small business)

With a huge global market, there are lots of options for where to host your crowdfunding project. Here are a few of the UK's most popular.

- **Crowdfunder** – currently 100 per cent free for fundraising in response to Covid-19

- **Crowdcube** – used by everyone from Monzo to tiny fledgling startups

- **Seedrs** – features Covid-19 support and £935.3 million in investment to date

- **Kickstarter** – specifically for creative projects and ideas

- **Indiegogo** – focused on early-adopter investment for new tech and design projects

Once you've picked your platform, you'll need to register your project. Remember, as well as registering, you're telling your audience about you, what you're trying to achieve and why their investment is so important, or valuable.

Hitting your target

Once your campaign's set up, it's time to promote it on social media, your email list and just about anywhere you have an engaged audience. Explain how their small donation is going to help you make your business better for them, as customers. Keep them up to date with how the fundraising's going, and drive momentum.

Remember, many crowdfunding websites or platforms take an all-or-nothing approach.

That means, if you don't hit your target, no money is paid. So it's worth going all-out on your other channels to raise awareness.

Where's the money?

Investors can pledge money at any point during your campaign, as long as it's within the timeframe you set from the start. Once you've hit the target and the campaign closes, your crowdfunding website will take a cut from the total amount raised.

You may also need to factor tax responsibilities into your crowdfunding plans. For example, reward and investment-based crowdfunding is usually classified as income, and may be subject to income and sales tax.

Do you pay back crowdfunding?

It depends on what kind of crowdfunding you're going for. With donation and reward-based crowdfunding, people are putting their money in for lots of different reasons – often through personal or social motivation – but not usually for a hard financial return.

Loan-based crowdfunding means that investors get their money back, usually with interest. And with investment-based crowdfunding, people put money in, usually for a share of your business. So they'll see the value of their shares rise and fall, but you don't need to pay back their investment.

Crowdfunding pros and cons – is it right for my business?

Here are a few of the biggest advantages that come with crowdfunding, plus some of the bug-bears:

It simplifies your pitching (and avoids the bank)

Traditionally, to secure investment and finance you'd probably need to hit a few different banks and potential investors, tailoring your pitch and plans accordingly. Crowdfunding means your campaign, details and progress are all hosted in one spot, for would-be investors to assess at their leisure.

Yes, you'll need to put targeted effort into promoting your crowdfunding to the right audience. But you won't be spending time preparing for pitch after pitch.

It's usually quick, with no upfront fees

You'll need to be organised, with somewhere other than your pitch for investors to go and get acquainted with your business. But once your campaign is live, you can raise funds relatively fast, without waiting out a lengthy decision process from a bank, for example. Many sites also feature no upfront fees for setting up and running your campaign, making the money even more accessible. But remember, fees and percentage cuts may apply once you've reached your target.

It gives an attention-grabbing story (and connected fanbase)

The nature of crowdfunding means that your investors are usually engaged with your project – more likely to click on your emails, for example, or stick with your product when loyalties are tested.

A great example is UK beer brand BrewDog, who've raised millions of pounds through innovative crowdfunding since launching in 2007. It's now a household name, but part of its secret is a huge community of super-loyal small-level investors, as passionate about the 'anti-business business model' as they are about the beer.

You need to be super-clear

With crowdfunding, you can't get on a Zoom meeting with a potential investor, look them in the eyes and explain your complex but brilliant project. Your online pitch space needs to be clear, attention-grabbing and easy to invest in, even if you're asking the audience to take a risk.

On the plus side, if it falls flat, you've secured some valuable market research and some platforms will let you ask for feedback.

It requires effort

Crowdfunding isn't just a case of signing up to a platform, handing over a few details and some nice wording about your project, posting it on social media and waiting for the money to start rolling in. You'll need to push it every step of the way, reminding people that time's running out, and maybe spend a bit of money on promotion, gearing up your website for higher traffic.

You'll also need to be on-hand to answer any questions, man your customer service or social media channels and let no scrap of engagement go to waste.

Finally – make crowdfunding work for your business

So now that you've secured your funding and have a new crowd of avid, excited followers and investors to boot, what next? Deliver, or disappoint. The harsh reality of crowdfunding is that you've set very public expectations, and failing to meet them or missing promised timescales will frustrate people, turn them off to the product, and put you in the firing line for bad publicity.

A good tactic here is to be really upfront, stay connected with your audience and share your journey with them. They'll be much more forgiving if they're up-to-date with your challenges, and excited for a product that'll be worth it in the end.

24 July 2020

Business success comes more from understanding life than enterprise

Entrepreneurs should aim to create a great company and, most of all, enjoy the job; people seldom run a business just to make money

By John Timpson

Q: One of my New Year's resolutions is to do more personal development. What skills do you think a small business owner with 25 employees should focus on?

A: By building a company that employs 25 people, you have graduated from the best business school in the world. Inexperienced MBAs may think they are trained professional managers, but the real pros are those who learn the lessons of experience by running their own enterprises.

Start by writing down why you have been successful, listing how and why you make money. Be honest; you probably had a few slices of luck along the way, but I expect your story will involve a good idea, some excellent colleagues and the determination to succeed.

Keep your business and life simple by understanding the key ingredients of your success. There's no need to embrace the new world of management with its big data, KPIs, dashboards, policies and process. Good business is seldom done by using buzzwords while attending "steering committees" on Zoom. You're close to your customers and should know all your colleagues – use this privileged position to your advantage.

You set the strategy, but let your team run the day-to-day business on your behalf. During 2021, make sure all your colleagues rate nine or 10 out of 10.

Start by learning how to help poor performers find their happiness elsewhere. You probably know two or three workers who are a drag on company performance, but you have failed to face up to the traumatic task of telling them they have to go.

If you really want a great business, make sure it's full of great people, which means saying goodbye to the passengers. It's unfair to expect dedicated colleagues to work alongside Mr Grumble and Mrs Late. Whenever one of these negative characters leaves, the whole organisation heaves a sigh of relief.

Try not to waste time on warning letters or performance management programmes – simply have a "part as friends" conversation. Be kind and generous, and remember: most of these poor performers don't enjoy working for you.

Dedicate the next 12 months to getting to know all your colleagues really well and find new ways to reward loyalty and exceptional performance.

At every Timpson leadership course, we ask participants to take the "How well do you know your people?" test. We ask questions about a member of their team: the name of their partner, the car they drive, the football team they support, children's names, favourite holiday destination and so on (we have already spoken to the team member to get the answers).

Great leaders know their colleagues well enough to know what rewards and birthday presents will be appreciated – and they recognise when things are going wrong. Great leadership includes mentoring colleagues through periods of personal stress. Divorce, money worries and bereavement can be the main reasons for a drop in performance.

Perhaps you think your principal role is to have imaginative ideas and make the big decisions, but if you have a great team, they will also have the ability to innovate and guide the business on your behalf. However, that's only if you trust them with the freedom to use their initiative.

Your biggest job is to create and develop the company culture. Learn to be the conductor of your orchestra. The musicians may play all the notes, but you make sure they're playing the same tune.

What else? Aim to make your job as easy as possible. A workforce of 25 doesn't require an elaborate management structure, but don't be tempted to do so many jobs yourself there's no time left to sit and think, or have a day off with your family. If you're responsible for sales, production, HR and finance, who runs the business when you are on holiday or ill? Develop your team by involving them in day-to-day management.

Aim to create a great enterprise and, most of all, enjoy your job; people seldom run a business just to make money. Life in business is more about understanding life than knowing about business.

11 January 2021

Sir John Timpson is chairman of the high-street services provider, Timpson.

5 common reasons stable businesses become insolvent

Whether your business is growing month after month or continuing to generate a stable amount of profit, poor habits and cash management can often cause it to go from stable and successful to insolvent in very little time.

Businesses become insolvent for a wide range of reasons. Some businesses face a cash flow crisis caused by customer non-payment, while others simply fail due to changes in market conditions or increased competition from other businesses.

Even if your business is doing well, it's important to understand that insolvency is always a possibility, and that taking steps to protect your business against it is an excellent idea.

As the old idiom states, it's best to "hope for the best, and prepare for the worst." By familiarising yourself with the most common causes for business insolvency, you'll be better able to protect your business from falling victim to them.

In this post, we'll examine five of the most common reasons stable, successful and profitable businesses become insolvent and how you can ensure your business is protected against them.

Cash flow crisis caused by limited funds

When your business earns tens or hundreds of thousands of pounds in profit every month, it's easy to assume that you can take a large amount of money out from the business without affecting its stability.

After all, next month's earnings will be enough to cover any unforeseen expenses or surprising bills, right? Not so. Sales can vary from one month to the next, and a small downturn could be all it takes to wipe you out if you don't have ample cash reserves.

Even if your business is doing extremely well and generating large profits, it's vital that you keep enough cash in your company's bank account to cover expenses such as payroll, inventory, production, rent, taxes and other essential costs.

Cash flow crises can occur on a moment's notice, especially if you haven't kept track of your company's expenses. A tax bill from HMRC for unpaid VAT could be all that's required to knock your successful, stable business off the financial rails.

The best way to avoid a cash flow crisis is to be prepared for any financial issue that could affect your business.

Keep enough cash in your company's account to cover its expenses and liabilities, even if doing so means slowing down its growth rate.

Loss of business from new competition

Have new competitors recently entered your industry? Competition isn't necessarily a bad thing for your business. In many cases, competitors validate that your market is worth operating in and help you make your business better.

However, ignoring your competitors, especially when they're growing rapidly, could lead to your business losing market share. This, in turn, can lead to declining profits and a lack of cash to operate your business effectively.

The best way to avoid losing market share to a competitor is by preparing ahead of time.

Study your competitors and understand their value proposition and benefits, then make sure your business offers better quality (or better value) than them.

It's also worth focusing on customer retention. Since your competitors will need to start from scratch, building a "moat" around your business by retaining customers will help you keep your revenue stable even if competition increases.

Loss/failure of an important customer

Is your business overly dependent on a single customer or client? If your business generates a large percentage of its profits from a single customer, it faces a serious risk of failure if the customer decides to switch to a competitor.

Likewise, the failure of an important customer or client – for example, a business bankruptcy for a B2B services client – could result in your company not receiving payment for its products or services.

This can be financially devastating, especially when your company offers a line of credit to its customers. Thankfully, the negative effects of losing a large customer can be mitigated by diversifying your business's sources of income.

Focus on acquiring new customers and clients that contribute a larger amount of income than the one large customer your business currently depends on. This will give you alternative sources of income in the event that a large customer fails.

Excessive debts and lack of stable sales

Have you borrowed heavily to build your business? Lots of businesses, from retail stores and restaurants to technology companies, depend on loans in order to build their product, rent retail property and start operating.

When your business is performing well, paying back debts and dealing with the cost of property rental is easy to manage. However, a single month of poor sales is often all it takes to cause your debt-related costs to exceed your monthly income.

Borrowing excessively places your business in a risky position – a single period of low sales can lead to its failure. Prepare ahead of time by keeping cash within your business to make up for temporary downturns in sales and revenue.

It's also important to minimise the amount of unnecessary debt your business takes on, especially in its early stages. Excessive debt creates vulnerabilities that can place your business in an insolvent position if its cash flow comes to a standstill.

Poor retention of important employees

Just like losing an important customer can lead to the failure of your business, losing an important employee can also lead to its decline. If your business is dependent on one or two key staff members, it's vulnerable in the event that it loses them.

Great businesses value key employees for their skills, knowledge and ability to help fuel growth and development. However, they never depend on individual members of staff, as this creates the risk of failure if multiple staff members leave at once.

Protect your business against the loss of key staff through preventative action. Look at the market salaries for staff members in important positions and ensure that your business is paying its key staff members what they're worth.

It's also important to pre-emptively mitigate the effects of losing a key staff member by ensuring your business isn't overly dependent on one person. Ensure that other members of staff are trained to take over in the event of a sudden departure.

While it's impossible to guarantee that an important staff member will stay with you for the long term, offering great compensation and ensuring they're happy with the role they occupy in your business will help your business maximise its retention.

Is your business at risk of becoming insolvent?

For many business owners and company directors, the idea of becoming insolvent is completely unthinkable. When you have steady revenue and strong profits, it seems impossible that your company could one day face a serious cash flow crisis.

However, many of the world's most profitable and successful businesses have faced cash flow issues and in some cases insolvency and bankruptcy with very little notice due to the loss of a key client or poor cash management.

If any of the above problems sound familiar to your business, it's important that you take action now to ensure they don't develop further. Preventative action is the best way to limit the risk of insolvency and ensure your business has a healthy future.

6 May 2020

Arcadia collapse: What does fall of Sir Philip Green's retail empire mean for its 13,000 workers?

Everything you need to know as Topshop and Dorothy Perkins owner goes into administration.

By Tom Embury-Dennis

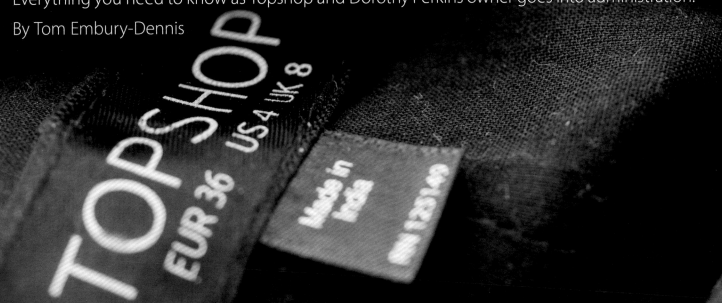

Sir Philip Green's Arcadia Group, which includes household names Topshop, Burton and Dorothy Perkins, has collapsed, putting around 13,000 jobs at risk.

The group, which has more than 500 stores across the UK, fell into administration after a last-minute multimillion-pound rescue deal involving Mike Ashley's Fraser Group fell through over the weekend.

Its collapse will see Deloitte appointed as administrators in the coming days and is set to trigger a scramble among creditors to gain control of the group's assets.

But what does it mean to go into administration, and what is it likely to mean for the company's thousands of employees?

What does Arcadia going into administration mean?

A firm goes into administration when it becomes insolvent; in effect when it becomes unable to pay its debts. At that point administrators take control of the business and will either force it into a restructuring, will sell the business or close it down and collect those debts.

In the case of Arcadia, sales have plummeted in recent months due to the coronavirus pandemic and its "material impact on trading", the company said.

To plug the gap in its finances, Arcadia launched emergency talks with lenders in an attempt to secure a £30m loan, but it emerged on Friday those talks had failed.

With it unable to now pay its lenders, administration represents the firm's last-ditch attempt to ward off creditors and potentially put in a restructuring plan.

Why is Arcadia struggling?

Even before the coronavirus pandemic, Arcadia's high-street names were struggling under a lack of investment and a failure to capitalise on the growing online market taken advantage of by brands such as Asos and Pretty Little Thing.

Guy Elliott, senior vice president at consultancy Publicis Sapient, said Arcadia's demise was not surprising after years of underinvestment.

"For the past few years, Arcadia and its brands have failed to be relevant to the demographics targeted by the respective brands, and Topshop in particular has lost much of its appeal to the younger generation," he said.

"I have no doubt that Topshop will be highly fought over as part of the administration process and hopefully new owners can turn it into the retail giant it once was, with the right investment in product, digital and marketing."

As well as Arcadia, rivals Debenhams, Edinburgh Woollen Mill Group and Oasis Warehouse have all also entered insolvency since the pandemic struck earlier this year.

What does this mean for its 13,000 employees?

As well as potentially losing their jobs, most of Arcadia's staff are also members of the company's pension fund, which has an estimated £350m hole in its finances.

Mirroring demands for Sir Philip to cover the £571m pension deficit left following his sale of BHS, Labour Party MP Stephen Timms on Friday called for the businessman to plug Arcadia's pension shortfall.

"Whatever happens to the group, the Green family must make good the deficit in the Arcadia pension fund," he said.

For now, Arcadia's stores are expected to continue trading through the Christmas period, meaning many staff will continue to work.

While some stores could ultimately close, the company's brands are likely to survive in some form as they are such household names.

But Arcadia already announced 500 redundancies at its head office earlier this year, and in 2019 creditors agreed a rescue deal that included rent reductions on its stores, 1,000 job cuts and dozens of store closures.

What does this mean for Sir Philip Green?

Public pressure on Sir Philip to cover any eventual shortfall in pensions is likely to be considerable.

In 2016, MPs passed a non-binding motion to strip the businessman of his knighthood following the collapse of BHS, which the previous year he sold to the serially bankrupt Dominic Chappell for £1.

Those demands died down after he covered the pension deficit, but a fresh crisis involving a new pensions fiasco and thousands of potential job losses could see those calls again grow louder.

And Sir Philip certainly has the money to cover any shortfall. He and his wife Lady Green are worth an estimated £930m, according to the Sunday Times Rich List.

Much of that wealth comes from when Sir Philip in 2005 paid himself £1.2bn in dividends from Arcadia, more than four times the company's pre-tax profit. The money went to his wife in Monaco, meaning it was not taxed in the UK.

While the tax payer largely supports Arcadia's workers through the furlough scheme, Sir Philip is reportedly planning a Christmas break at a luxury resort in the Maldives where private villas cost up to £30,000-a-night.

20 November 2020

The factors behind Arcadia's collapse

Drapers looks at three challenges that derailed Sir Philip Green's Arcadia Group.

By Emily Sutherland

Think back to the spring of 2007. Sir Philip Green is sipping champagne alongside Kate Moss at Topshop's giant Oxford Street store, celebrating the model's successful collaboration with what was then one of the high street's coolest names. Hordes of shoppers queued around the block to get their hands on the range. Topshop was beloved by fashion fans – regardless of age or budget – for its ability to deliver a reasonably priced style bargain. Green's business empire seemed unbreakable.

The intervening years have been tough on the retail industry, and on Arcadia, and the Covid-19 pandemic has accelerated its decline. The group, which also includes Miss Selfridge, Dorothy Perkins, Topman, Evans, Wallis, Outfit and Burton, collapsed into administration on Monday evening. Drapers analyses what went wrong at what was once the high street's biggest success story.

"The level of competition for customer spend is almost awe-inducing."

Competition

The retail landscape today bears little resemblance to the world when the Arcadia Group was at its peak. Topshop, the jewel of the group's crown, faces a plethora of competition from newer names with slicker online operations or a more distinct brand handwriting.

The level of competition for customer spend is almost awe-inducing – Topshop is jostling for space alongside Spanish giant Zara, known for its tech savvy and breathtakingly speedy takes on catwalk styles; the ever-expanding Boohoo Group, to which social media and trends come naturally; and a plethora of well-executed brands from H&M Group, including flagship fascia H&M, & Other Stories and Weekday.

And then there's Asos. The online pureplay has hoovered up Topshop's market share, growing as Green's Arcadia shrinks. Today's young shoppers are much more likely to browse Asos or Boohoo's permanently refreshed new-in pages when there's money burning a hole in their pockets than they are to visit their local Topshop store.

Increased competition has knocked Topshop off its perch and proved disastrous for Miss Selfridge, Dorothy Perkins and Wallis, which already suffered from less distinctive handwriting. They were easily lost in fashion's ever-expanding crowd.

Arcadia's status in the UK clothing market has plummeted. In 2015, it was the fourth biggest fashion retailer, but this year it has fallen to 10th place, falling by 1.8% to hold just 2.7% of the market, research firm GlobalData reports.

Competition on price is another factor in the Arcadia Group's decline. Topshop and its sister brands sit firmly in fashion's squeezed middle. H&M, Boohoo, Primark, PrettyLittleThing and Zara all offer shoppers a cheaper alternative. Many of

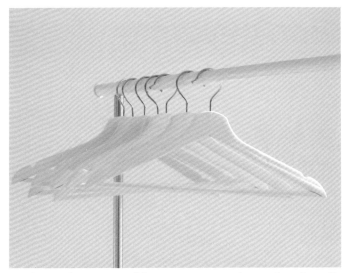

Boohoo's dresses retail for £20-£30 – and are often heavily discounted – compared with Topshop's £30-£40.

Price is a key consideration in today's market, and the Arcadia Group's brands have been overtaken in value for money.

"Cracks in the Arcadia Group have become chasms as a result of the pandemic."

Covid-19

Things were far from rosy at the Arcadia Group long before the Covid-19 pandemic turned life upside down. Creditors approved seven company voluntary arrangements from the Arcadia Group in June last year, which resulted in the closure of 23 stores. The group also closed six Miss Selfridge stores and 19 Evans stores the same year after it put two property subsidiaries into administration. All 11 Topshop/Topman stores in the US were closed and the group's majority shareholder, Lady Tina Green, invested a further £50m into the business, on top of the £50m she had previously invested earlier that year.

In September 2019, the group reported an operating loss of £138m for the 53 weeks to 1 September 2018 – the first time in seven years it had fallen into the red – and admitted it might require yet more additional funding to turn things around. Arcadia Group blamed a tough trading environment for the troubles it was facing at the time, but the business could not have imagined then just how much more difficult things would get.

The pandemic, repeated lockdowns, economic uncertainty and a complete dearth of any social events to buy new clothes for has shaken even fashion's strongest businesses to their core.

The group axed 500 roles in July as the coronavirus crisis took a toll on sales, arguing its digital platforms had not been able to make up the sales shortfall from shuttered stores.

In September, the business was also forced to back down on its decision not to pay furloughed staff their full salaries during their notice periods, admitting it had "got this decision wrong".

Cracks in Arcadia have become chasms as a result of the pandemic. Life may be expected to return to something closer to normality by next spring, but that still leaves struggling retail businesses facing at least another five months of stagnant sales. Even then, consumers are likely to be extremely price conscious for the foreseeable future, and reign back on discretionary spending. It will take two years for the fashion industry's revenue to recover to 2019 levels, according to a recent report from management consultants McKinsey, meaning many businesses are facing a bleak future.

Costs

Unlike younger entrants to the fashion landscape, the Arcadia Group has a large and expensive store estate. Despite its 2019 CVA, the retail group still has hundreds of stores on high streets and in shopping centres – two destinations badly hurt by the pandemic.

Newer fashion players – such as Boohoo Group and Asos – tend to have no stores, or focus on a handful of units in key locations.

The days of having a bricks-and-mortar presence on every high street are gone, and businesses still reliant on that model of retail are struggling. High rents and crippling business rates have made bricks-and-mortar an expensive proposition.

There will be a place for stores when the dust from the pandemic clears, but they must offer customers something special. The Arcadia Group's model of copycat stores needs revisiting. But this is a business that does understand retail theatre – Topshop's Oxford Street store remains a destination thanks to the events and experiences on offer there, and could be a blueprint for the brand's bricks-and-mortar presence in the future. However, significant investment is essential.

Controversy

Green's retail empire has crumbled as his reputation for controversy has grown. First, there was BHS. The businessman sold the ailing department store to Dominic Chappell, who had little retail experience and had previously gone bankrupt, for £1 in 2015. BHS collapsed less than a year later, resulting the loss of 11,000 jobs and a £571m pension deficit. Green agreed a £363m cash settlement with the Pensions Regulator in 2017, but his reputation was tarnished by the saga.

More recently, Green has faced allegations of bullying, abusive behaviour and sexual harassment. In 2018, he was named as the British businessman behind an injunction against the Daily Telegraph, which stopped the newspaper naming him in a report unveiling sexist and racist behaviour.

The allegations have sat poorly with customers as shoppers' interest in businesses' values and ethics has skyrocketed over recent months, giving consumers another reason to avoid Arcadia's brands.

30 November 2020

Inspiring a new generation of young entrepreneurs

By Emma Jones - Founder, Enterprise Nation

Record numbers of people are becoming their own boss in the UK. More than 400,000 people have already formed a company in 2019, and the UK is on track to reach the milestone of over half a million people starting a business within the space of a year for the sixth year running.

The appetite for entrepreneurship is alive and well, and young people can take their fair share of responsibility for this boom. Surveys show that more than 60% of young people say they want to be their own boss. On leaving school, colleges, universities and jobs, young people are taking their passion for music, dance, tech, food, or whatever else their interest might be and basing a business on it. Many are starting as side hustles and running a business alongside a day job, studies, or travel.

Our job at Enterprise Nation is to support these young businesses and represent their views. Based on what we hear every day from young people participating in our Next Generation campaign, we've created a 6 point list to help us make sure the next decade offers the ideal conditions for young people to thrive.

It all starts at school

There is great work underway to make sure young people get exposure to enterprise in school. Students can learn about business through the work of the Careers and Enterprise Company with its national network of enterprise advisers and competitions such as Tenner Challenge. There are also organisations like Founders4Schools who connect business people with schools. This work could be strengthened if enterprise formed part of the school curriculum.

Make the connections

Young people have a strong understanding of how to use technology to build a business, which is a vital skill in 2019. But what they often lack (purely due to age) is a strong network of supporters in the form of peers, mentors and advisers.

Experienced entrepreneurs tend not to hang out in the same spaces and places as young start-ups. We'd love to see a network that could connect business people of all ages for equal support. It's something we're looking to develop at Enterprise Nation, but it does depend on the willingness of more mature entrepreneurs to offer time to guide the next generation - which can be tough when you have a business of your own to run.

Showcase role models

There is a well-known saying when it comes to supporting young people: "You can't be what you can't see". This means role models are of paramount importance. Recent young entrepreneurs such as Jamal Edwards, Steve Bartlett and Rose Dyson have become such role models and we'd love to see a spotlight shone on more enterprising individuals.

Access to cash

Another resource young people lack is funding, simply because they haven't had time to save and store reserves. We've been working with TSB regional managers to support young people with business planning, and we're also involved with funders such as The Prince's Trust and StartUp Loans.

The rise of crowdfunding has plugged a funding gap, but we would welcome more funding for young people who have minimal trading records and can be considered higher risk. Organisations offering small amounts of test funding and business support could give young people the best opportunity to take the initial steps. After that, your confidence and network will grow along with your ability to raise follow-on funds.

Superfast connectivity

The new Prime Minister has expressed a strong commitment to the roll-out of superfast broadband. This will be music

to the ears of young entrepreneurs, but many will also be welcoming 5G and considering the art of what's possible. We look forward to 5G spurring yet more tech innovation among young founders.

Resilience

Possibly the most vital asset any entrepreneur will need throughout their journey is resilience. This comes from having a positive state of mind and being surrounded by supporters who help to build the strength and energy required to keep going when times are tough. This is why we need to surround our young entrepreneurs with support from the outset.

If we continue to work on these points in the UK, I'm convinced we'll make the most of the amazing talent of young people and the entrepreneurial opportunities that lie ahead. We will be a better country for it.

Emma Jones is the founder of small business support company, Enterprise Nation.

30 August 2019

Five young entrepreneurs from Scotland win national award

Nina Birchard, Lucy Fisher, Elena Höge, Iona Mackenzie and Petra Baiba Olehno have started the new year with a boost.

From: Office of the Secretary of State for Scotland, UK Research and Innovation, and Iain Stewart MP

Five of this year's Young Innovator Award winners, announced today by Innovate UK and The Prince's Trust, are from Scotland. The winners will receive a £5,000 grant, one-on-one business coaching and an allowance to cover living costs.

The Scottish innovators looking to make the world a better place are:

Nina Birchard, 24, Glasgow, who has designed the Newborn Rescue Towel, a low cost emergency medical device which provides thermal support and the correct positioning to aid resuscitation in newborns.

Lucy Fisher, 25, Aberdeen, who has taken a childhood passion for knitting and turned it into a business. Knit It aims to bring knitting into the 21st century via a new digital platform which enables knitters to have a choice in how they follow a pattern and guides them through creating their new designs.

Elena Höge, 28, Edinburgh, who is creating educational games like Wholesome, a mobile forest school experience that teaches children and adults about nature, including how to forage and cook with wild food.

Iona Mackenzie, 26, Edinburgh, whose Talk and Grow business aims to take the stress out of finding a therapist for those in need of support in Edinburgh with an online matching and booking platform to pair clients with a number of local counsellors.

Petra Baiba Olehno, 30, a Glasgow-based Latvian who wants to create REPAIREL, a one-stop-shop for buying ethical footwear online which allows people to compare information about shoes and brands.

The Young Innovators Awards recognise young people from across the UK with great business ideas who have the potential to become successful entrepreneurs and future leaders in innovation.

Following an unprecedented level of entries, with an 87% increase in applications year-on-year, 64 young people have started the New Year with a boost after getting the coveted award, double the number of award winners/recipients of previous years.

With recent research showing over a third of 18 to 34 year olds want to launch an independent enterprise in 2021, compared to 28% of 35 to 54 year olds, it's even more important the support is available to those who want to venture into starting a business.

The winners from Scotland are five of 64 inspiring young people who will receive Young Innovators Awards this year, each benefitting from a £5,000 grant, one-on-one business coaching and an allowance to cover living costs. The programme is set to continue awarding young people from diverse backgrounds until at least 2023. This year, 49% of the winners are female; nearly a third are Black, Asian or from an ethnic minority background; 17% have a disability and the projects cover all regions across the UK.

From a way to help stroke survivors on the road to rehabilitation to support for parents to protect their children online, all of this year's Young Innovators have ideas that promise to address current challenges. Ideas this year span everything from technology to physical and mental health and from sustainability to fashion.

13 January 2021

Why big businesses move their headquarters around the world – tax, talent and trepidation

An article from The Conversation.

THE CONVERSATION

By Carmen Raluca Stolan, Lecturer in International Business, University of Kent

Ever since the EU referendum of 2016, well-known companies have announced decisions to relocate outside of the UK. Electronic giant Panasonic has gone to Amsterdam, where Sony will soon follow. Ferry company P&O will shift registration of its vessels to Cyprus, while the engineering firm Dyson is moving its corporate headquarters to Singapore.

There is nothing new about big businesses relocating their corporate headquarters. Back in 2003 the United Nations Conference on Trade and Development was hailing the arrival of a world market for such possibilities. And even iconic American companies have decided to move, including Burger King (to Canada), Budweiser (to Belgium), and Lucky Strike (to the UK). So why do they do it? And what are the benefits of moving?

One of the most obvious and compelling reasons to move is the desire to increase profits. There can be huge tax breaks associated with being a legal entity registered in a tax haven. Ireland, Switzerland and Panama have all attracted this kind of investment.

But a move like this comes with potential costs however. Companies risk damage to their reputation – including accusations of tax avoidance and unethical behaviour, while the countries they move to face increased scrutiny.

Another reason to relocate is to base the business in a major financial centre such as London, New York, Frankfurt or Hong Kong. Firms that do this may be motivated by better opportunities to raise capital and have access to highly specialised talent. This kind of move is particularly popular with businesses from emerging economies as it shows a commitment to robust legal standards and business practices. This can enhance their reputation (and subsequently, performance).

Finally, businesses sometimes relocate as a result of an acquisition. When a company is bought up by another company, its corporate location may switch to that of the buyer – this is what happened when Budweiser moved to Belgium, after it was bought by InBev.

Yet despite all these motives to relocate, for many multinationals there is no place like home. This could be because it is where the founder is from, and where they managed to provide a solution to a business problem which existed in that country – where an entire ecosystem crucial for setting up the business exists, and where the main stakeholders are.

So when a relocation of a corporate headquarters happens, as in the case of Dyson and P&O, push factors may be at play too. Some corporations decide to relocate when the home

country ecosystem that has made them competitive in the first place is damaged, and the perceived advantages of a new home market are higher than the perceived advantages of their country of origin.

This is where Brexit clearly matters for many businesses that have their corporate headquarters in the UK. When uncertainty strikes, when there are worries about attracting talent, when the legislative regime is unclear and the quality of the services available is under threat, the issue of where the headquarters should be located becomes salient.

Why worry?

The economic impact of relocation varies. Some corporate headquarters have very limited functions and only a limited number of staff, while others are larger employers, so the job losses differ from case to case. Nevertheless, the jobs that are relocated are usually highly skilled, specialised jobs that are very well paid and often highly taxed. Corporate tax revenue losses may also be significant.

Also, the economic impact goes far beyond the company itself. A relocation can lessen demand for highly specialised services such as legal advice, banking, and logistics – all of which have a negative effect on the economic ecosystem of the home country and its ability to attract future investors.

Last but not least, relocation is highly symbolic. While some businesses choose to relocate to show a commitment to a new region (where arguably their most important customers and competitors are) this move surely sends the opposite message to their former home country – a country that no longer fully meets the needs of an investor with global ambitions.

Investor confidence is crucial to make or break an investment destination, and investors often follow the decisions of others. With the continuing uncertainty of Brexit, it is likely that more companies will decide to relocate. Those who set up their regional headquarters in the UK as a stepping stone for further expansion in the EU will be no doubt be thinking of a change, while many EU governments are doing their best to lure them away.

Amsterdam has already snapped up Sony and Panasonic through its location, competitiveness and excellent quality of life. Dublin is hoping to appeal to US investors through the shared language, historical links between the two countries, a welcoming investment climate and tax breaks. Berlin, the new start-up capital of Europe, is trying to attract UK entrepreneurs with its low set-up costs, good higher education institutes and infrastructure, as well as a young and diverse talent pool. Paris is aiming to lure international banks away from the City of London by easing regulation.

Soon after the EU referendum, a KPMG survey showed that 76% of the 1,300 CEOs surveyed around the world were looking to relocate the headquarters of their firms. Although some of the CEOs' opinions may have changed since then, there has certainly been a recent trend in moving headquarters away from the UK. If too many companies decide to join them, there will be worrying times for those left behind.

22 February 2019

2020 the year of HSCR - Honest Corporate Social Responsibility

By Jamie Mackenzie

While the powerful descend on Switzerland for the Davos Summit in January 2020, determined to show their new concern for climate change, the likelihood is that they'll then fly back home on their private jets demonstrating how CSR credentials are hard to earn, but even easier to tarnish.

We can all point to a business that claims that the principles of diversity and inclusion are integral to everything they do – while their C-suite is populated entirely with white, middle-class men. Or the firm that brags about its concern for the rainforest, press-releasing its commitment to planting hundreds of trees in Brazil, whilst conducting all its operations on paper. Not to mention the company that espouses support for various charitable initiatives whilst failing to offer volunteering leave for its staff.

In this context perhaps it is not surprising that according to a World Value Index survey, only 14% of employees say their values are well-aligned with the companies for which they work and – when it comes to CSR – nearly a third think that corporations only support specific causes to make themselves look good or accrue tax benefits.

Adding the honesty factor to corporate social responsibility (CSR) is so important. It means neutralising criticism whilst winning hearts and minds by stating up front: "We're doing our best, but we've got a long way to go." Ultimately, businesses have to make money – otherwise they won't survive so it's best to admit that whilst also demonstrating a commitment to doing so as ethically as possible. Transparency is vital and there should be clear and regular reporting both internally and externally to make sure every member of the workforce feels heard.

People must be at the heart of any corporate responsibility approach. Rather than aiming too high, companies should look at fostering employee engagement – offering incentive programmes that successfully integrate corporate values and leverage CSR as an employee reward. This could include facilitating the desire of particular individuals who want to carry out charity work over charitable giving.

After all, so many charities have been exposed as mis-using funds in recent years – exhibiting the very opposite of this 'honest' aesthetic. If management is able to integrate HCSR into their staff recognition schemes then the business rewards could be not only endearing but profound too.

'Doing good' is becoming increasingly important when it comes to achieving business success. Research from Sodexo Engage shows that 87% of employees believe that the success of a business should be measured in terms of more than just its financial performance and 64% would not take a job if a potential employer did not take CSR seriously. Ultimately, focusing on that simple word 'honesty' will pay dividends – it's important for us all to realise that though a great leap forward may be the dream, in reality progress is implemented step by step.

20 December 2019

B Corp certification won't guarantee companies really care for people, planet and profit

THE CONVERSATION

An article from The Conversation.

By Michael O'Regan, Senior Lecturer in Events & Leisure, Bournemouth University

Weeks after the collapse of his restaurant group and the loss of 1,000 jobs, celebrity chef Jamie Oliver announced that he was creating an "ethical" B Corporation or "B Corp", a sort of company certification designed to show its holder gives equal weight to people, planet and profit. While it has loosely the same aim as the "triple bottom line" of the social enterprise model, B Corp certification is available to for-profit companies that apply to B Lab, a non-global profit organisation, and pay for it.

B Lab was founded in 2006 by Stanford University alumni and businessmen Jay Coen Gilbert and Bart Houlahan, and former investment banker and Stanford colleague, Andrew Kassoy. There are now more than 2,900 certified B Corps in more than 60 countries, cutting across industries and sectors. Through extensive lobbying and promotion it has expanded worldwide through new local offices. With the number of B Corps opening under the organisation's UK arm growing at 14% a year, is this really a new way of doing business?

People, planet and profit

On the face of it, the certification should indicate a company's environmental performance, employee relationships, diversity, involvement in the local community, and the impact a company's product or service has on those it serves. This in turn can attract staff and consumers seeking socially responsible businesses, boost an established public company's stock price, and help investors find companies that balance profit and purpose.

In the B Lab certification process, a businesses must sign a "Declaration of Interdependence", committing it to using "business as a force for good". The company must modify its governing bylaws to allow directors to "consider stakeholders besides shareholders in company decision-making". Companies must also disclose information on "any sensitive practices, fines, and sanctions related to the company or its partners". Certification is done chiefly over the phone, with around 10% selected for more in-depth review. Companies must re-certify every three years.

Chapter 2: Corporate Responsibility

While B Corp claims that certification balances the interests of shareholders with the interests of workers, customers, communities and the environment, B Corp standards are not legally enforceable. Neither the board nor the corporation are liable for damages if a company fails to meet them. Even the changes in company bylaws remain secret. A business can fill out the initial B Corp Impact Assessment in a few hours, and complete the certification process in between four and eight weeks, finally paying a certification fee of between US$500 and US$50,000, depending on revenue.

B Corp certification is available to any for-profit business around the globe as long as it's been operating for at least 12 months. Certification is initially self-assessed, and doesn't override the profit-driven focus of the company.

A cash-generating machine?

B Lab has raised over US$32m since launch, and receives much of its funding from major foundations and organisations such as Prudential, Deloitte LLP, the Rockefeller Foundation, and even the US Agency for International Development. In 2017 it received about US$6m in certification fees, and US$5.6m in donations. Its board members primarily come from the business sector, with B Lab paying US$6m in salaries and compensation in 2017.

In the face of this highly cash-generative activity, B Lab's rhetoric ("lead a movement") fails to spell out compelling reasons for certification. B Lab claims that traditional corporations cannot be socially responsible, because they open themselves to liability for not following shareholders' interests. But there is no law that explicitly requires directors of businesses to maximise shareholder revenue to the exclusion of all other corporate objectives. European (EU Directive 2014/95/EU) and UK law already push companies to practise sustainability reporting, and British firms have always had the flexibility to amend their articles of association with shareholder consent to reflect their social responsibilities. Pharmaceutical company Novo Nordisk, for example, changed its Articles of Association to state that it "strives to conduct its activities in a financially, environmentally and socially responsible way".

So while B Lab speaks of seeking to meet the "highest standards of verified social and environmental performance, public transparency, and legal accountability to balance profit and purpose" it has nevertheless certified companies allegedly involved in tax avoidance, those producing cannabis-related products, for-profit college education companies, corporations working in the prison sector, and those allegedly involved in union busting.

What value does it add?

My research into one of the earliest certified B Corps, CouchSurfing.com, shows how certification can be used to pacify angry consumers and attract investors. Certified companies can simply walk away if they feel being a B Corp no longer suits their profit-making aims or strategy, or if it threatens short-term shareholder profitability. The online marketplace Etsy is one that walked away, while others dropped certification after being bought out by larger companies that had other plans.

There is no directory of former B Corporations that dropped certification or had it removed. The closed nature of a private certifying body that sets and regulates its own standards is problematic, even if well intentioned, and especially so if it seeks to control the process by which certified businesses are held accountable. Certified corporations are as accountable to B Lab as they are to their stakeholders. The lack of full transparency and rigorous vetting in the face of its aggressive expansion indicates that B Lab's certification should not be seen as a reliable method for certifying corporations to some standard, from the perspective of either the general public, investors or regulators.

Which isn't to say that the efforts haven't been worthwhile. B Lab could re-focus and promote new global benchmarks and corporate structures such as low-profit limited liability companies (L3Cs) in the US, or community interest companies (CICs) and multi-stakeholder co-operatives in the UK. Rather than striving to become a political-economic actor spending millions on creating and marketing a private company certification offering brand building and expensive workshops, B Lab might consider whether its market-driven certification offers solutions to market-produced problems.

Jamie Oliver is largely transparent in his business values and commitment to social responsibility. He would be better to say "goodbye and big love as ever" to B Lab as he did in his goodbye letter to staff, and focus instead on working with co-operatives, worker and community-owned businesses, and other non-profits that are building a new economy now – without the need to buy a certificate.

7 October 2019

Inside the corporate world's great diversity and inclusion project

Corporate diversity programmes are rising—and have become a flashpoint in the culture wars. But are they working?

By Rebecca Liu

In 2017, the Parker Review, an independent government-backed report, laid down a simple challenge to Britain's FTSE 100 companies: to appoint at least one—"just one"—director from an ethnic minority background by the end of 2021, with a slightly more distant deadline of 2024 for smaller FTSE 250 boards.

The report had discovered that over 50 per cent of FTSE 100 companies had no ethnic minority directors. Black, Asian and minority ethnic (BAME) board members made up just 8 per cent of the UK's total, while the UK BAME population is 14 per cent. But even worse, if you only consider British BAME citizens, thereby excluding investors and high-flyers jetted in from elsewhere, the number plummeted to 2 per cent. What's more, minority directors are clustered in a few firms, often with specific Asian and African connections: just seven companies in the UK contained 40 per cent of the nation's BAME directors. "The boardrooms of Britain's leading public companies do not reflect the ethnic diversity of either the UK or the stakeholders that they seek to engage and represent," the Review concluded.

Progress was tracked in an updated 2020 Parker Review earlier this year, and it appeared wanting. Out of the 256 companies with meaningful data, 150—or 59 per cent—had yet to appoint a BAME board member. A similar report by the recruitment consultancy Green Park in 2019 found that the number of BAME board members decreased to 7.4 per cent from 2018's 9 per cent.

It is fashionable in some corners to dismiss campaigners on these issues as irritatingly "woke," but before doing so we should look at the bald statistics—and listen to the experiences of those in Britain's workplaces. A 2019 study by the TUC found that over 70 per cent of ethnic minority workers have experienced racial harassment at work; a 2020 YouGov survey found that 84 per cent of Britain's BAME citizens think the UK is "very" or "somewhat" racist; while a 2019 Oxford analysis that involved sending identical CVs and covering letters to 3,200 employers discovered that applicants with ethnic minority-sounding names needed to make 60 per cent more applications to get the same number of call backs as applicants with white British ones.

The Parker Review's recommendations follow similar government initiatives to improve female board representation, which have borne more fruit: women now hold a historic third of positions across the UK's major companies, meeting targets a year ahead of schedule. But with race we have seen an articulation of good intentions, followed by government-backed targets, only to end up with statistics that barely move—or slide back. Worries about ethnic minority representation in top positions have broad repercussions: a lack of diversity in Britain's top firms will mean fewer personal connections with Asia, Africa and beyond, which could hamper attempts to build the non-European trade links that Boris Johnson's government insists are essential to post-Brexit prosperity. Over the summer, with the resurgence of the Black Lives Matter movement, many companies were prompted to reconsider the state of racial equality in their own workplaces. Some institutions are trying to take the initiative for the first time, but—with grim inevitability—programmes like "unconscious bias" training have become a flashpoint in the culture wars. In September, 40 Conservative MPs publicly refused to participate in such training sessions; a few days later, Donald Trump issued an executive order that forbade US government vendors from "divisive" diversity training.

Trump is on his way out, and the fury could settle down, but the deeper concern is whether diversity training is worth it. Beyond the landmark reports, static statistics, and big PR splashes, the UK's diversity and inclusion (D&I) business is flowering, with more D&I officers being appointed, more unconscious bias sessions and other initiatives growing by the day. But are such programmes really doing any good?

***

In the TV show Succession, a white graduate attends his first day of work at an American media empire (an internship he got through nepotism: he's the grandnephew of the CEO). He scarfs down a sandwich at his desk while watching an introductory video. "The company is committed to making employment decisions without regard to race, religion, creed, gender," a robotic woman's voice announces, set against footage of ethnically diverse professional-looking women and men smiling and laughing. The camera pans away from the video and across to the real office, where a group of employees are leaving a meeting room. They are all middle-aged white men.

Corporate diversity efforts have often aroused suspicions that they are nothing but a cynical box-ticking exercise. Ben (not his real name) is a consultant at an international firm with projects across Asia and Africa, and one of the few BAME senior staffers at his majority white office. For him, diversity was often addressed through annual training featuring "clunky videos about workplace behaviour, harassment and racism." Much like Succession's intern, Ben and his colleagues would skip through the exercises unenthusiastically: "You'd click through some of them and the ones you couldn't skip, you'd do. After a while everyone just clicks through."

The roots of the modern diversity programme go back to the rejection of biological racism after the Second World War. In the subsequent decades, new thinking about industrial relations came to regard the workplace as host to important social and psychological dynamics, as business historian Kira Lussier told me. She pointed me to the pioneering role of black American psychiatrist Price Cobbs. Cobbs, the author of Black Rage (1968), an influential study of the anger and trauma caused by racism and the legacy of slavery, used his expertise in what he called "ethnotherapy" to consult for companies on racial integration in the workplace.

But the real boom in corporate diversity training came as a result of anti-discrimination laws, and the threat of expensive lawsuits and bad press. In Diversity Inc: The Failed Promise of a Billion-Dollar Business, Pamela Newkirk observes the landmark $192.5m racial discrimination case settled by Coca Cola and its 2,200 black employees in 2000. Citing the 1964 Civil Rights Act, plaintiffs argued that the company had discriminated against them in regard to promotions, pay, and performance evaluations. The settlement, "the largest for racial discrimination in legal history," sparked a hiring drive in D&I officers within a newly wary corporate America. Earlier rulings, such as the class action suit at Xerox in the 1970s, also mandated companies to offer diversity training. The birth of D&I in the multinational corporate world was tied to legal compliance, with the aim of preserving reputations and the bottom line, rather than any high-flown ideals about racial justice.

In the UK, similar protections have been enshrined over many decades, starting with the extension, in 1968, of the first Race Relations Act to cover employment. The framework was toughened up in the 1970s, and then more recently through the 2010 Equality Act. When Jennie O'Reilly—director at consultancy Steps Drama, whose clients include BAE Systems, IBM and Tesco—first began working in diversity training in 2008, the focus was predominantly around legal compliance. Sessions were about "what was OK, not OK, and far more aligned to what the law said," O'Reilly tells me. Now, she observes, companies are increasingly concerned about culture and belonging. "It's less about misconduct and more about what are the biases and behaviours that we hold," she said. Her firm uses actors to perform scenes that touch on issues within company culture: a woman returning from maternity leave being talked down to by her boss, for example. Attendees watch, discuss and debate the scenarios. In the past, O'Reilly said, sessions were about "teaching that the law says it isn't OK for you to do this; now we were saying 'what does it feel like to you, if you were that person up there, experiencing that?'"

***

On a rainy Wednesday afternoon this autumn, I logged onto a Steps taster course in "allyship," focusing on how members of advantaged groups can support those who find themselves on the wrong side of prejudice or discrimination. The course was a free 90-minute session open to the public and capped at 30 attendees. My screen soon filled with 25 others, predominantly from the US and UK. The group contained a mix of genders and races; what it did not appear to include were many younger people. Four Steps facilitators had also logged in, as well as a number of silent observing staff. We were put into three smaller discussion "groups," assisted by Zoom's "breakout room" function, to meet and chat with other participants for five minutes.

Once we returned, a brief overview of key concepts was provided by Joe (not his real name), a cheery lead facilitator. Definitions of "institutional racism" and "white privilege" were shown on PowerPoint slides. Discussions of these complex concepts were held at a quick pace: Joe explained privilege was about what you don't have to experience, and thus can easily miss. No one intervened with any objections, suggesting that people who volunteer to spend an afternoon in allyship training might not be the ones most in need of it. Then came Steps' drama offering: a scenario involving a heated debate between two senior employees and their manager at a law firm. The scene was acted out with verve across three Zoom windows.

Joe played Andy, the manager. Andy was talking to two members of staff—Nate, who was white, and Kareem, who was black. The trio were putting together a team for a new client. Kareem advocated for a young black lawyer in their firm to be given a chance; Andy cut in and said that the company was "in crisis mode" and not in a position to take risks. He went for their usual go-to legal team. Andy declared the meeting over and asked Kareem to assemble the team. When Andy left, Nate, previously quiet in the discussion, turned to Kareem and said: "by the way, I agreed with you."

We were divided back into our smaller "rooms" to discuss, before finally coming together in an all-team appraisal. In the ensuing debate, participants were quick to support Kareem, suggesting that he find other allies in the office. Nate was advised to stand with Kareem in a more productive way—by saying he agreed after the event, people observed, he was rubbing salt in the wound. Many white participants focused on how Nate might develop the courage to stand up to Andy next time. But hang on, a black participant asked: are you actually interested in helping Kareem or do you merely want to look like you're helping? A spirited discussion about the line between being a self-indulgent saviour and a genuine ally followed. Most of the energy in the room, however, was reserved for Andy. Listen to your employees Andy, exclaimed the participants, often older white men. One edged towards disagreement, contending that sometimes the boss has to make the final call. Others pointed to how the scenario restaged a common problem faced by BAME employees in elite spaces: they are likely to be in junior positions, and thereby unable to do much to reset the balance, a vicious cycle of disadvantage.

I left the session invigorated, though it is clear that a 90-minute discussion can hardly transform someone with longstanding prejudices into a committed anti-racist—let alone equip them with the skills to push through organisational change. (Steps' usual offering is more long term, O'Reilly told me, involving a research phase, and a post-course monitoring phase lasting up to a year.) The value of that session was not so much in the transmission of the kind of "critical race theory" that Conservative equalities minister Kemi Badenoch rails against in parliament, but rather in giving people from different walks of life an opportunity to

speak, disagree and learn from one another. Ideally, it would not only be in earmarked training sessions where such discussions could be possible. A healthy workplace should be facilitating them as a matter of course.

Such training sessions can vary greatly in form. Others I spoke to have attended sessions with quick-fire "check your privilege" rounds in which participants list the number of BAME friends they have; sessions that involve "identify the stereotype" exercises (which could, without care, merely reinforce biases); and PowerPoints that lay out the meaning, causes and effects of racial stereotyping. Reactions to these sessions range from appreciation and greater edification to bafflement, anger and further entrenchment of biases.

Diversity Inc's Pamela Newkirk told me that some anti-bias training can fuel resentment among white men—we shouldn't forget that Trump still got over 73m votes in November's election. There is a job to do here, but it requires professional skill. The D&I industry, Raj Tulsiani, CEO of Green Park, told me, is full of people with no formal qualifications. The industry's lack of rigour and resources is aggravated by the fact that D&I is still seen by many as "nice to have" rather than essential. "If it were any other business problem, it would be something that people were really serious about," he said. But the sheer fact that it isn't a priority means that companies cut corners, relying on crude "cut-and-paste" models. More important than any course, Newkirk added, is for a company to take responsibility for how its own practices have caused "racially unequal pay, opportunity, promotions."

***

The 2017 landmark McGregor-Smith Review on race in the workplace recommends a six-phase roadmap that includes data gathering, setting and chasing targets, asking senior leadership to be accountable, raising awareness among employees—that's where training comes in—examining recruitment policies and installing transparency around reward and recognition. For Sue (not her real name), a mid-level analyst at a global investment bank, seeing other east Asian women in senior leadership positions gives her faith that D&I is taken seriously daily—and offers her a model to advance her own career. Change, she affirms, starts from the top: "if people higher up push for it, then you strive for it." Additionally, though filling in questionnaires about your racial identity is alienating for some, Mary Agbesanwa, management consultant at PwC and winner of the 2020 EMpower Ethnic Minority Future Leader award, finds that data on team composition and attrition rates can reveal "how big of an issue it is… otherwise you don't really know"; to discover crucial data is to "convince leadership of the issue." Tracking progress, or lack thereof, in racial representation in the corporate sector is often hampered by the lack of such data: the first Parker Review found that only half of the FTSE 100 companies asked for figures were able to share "any meaningful information."

Disagreement about solutions abounds. Some firms have touted that they hire using name-blind CVs. But, Tulsiani counters, "why should I have to hide my identity to come work for you?", pointing out that if someone's name makes them less likely to be hired, then the same issue might arise come "promotion and bonus time." Then there is the issue of diversity work "trapping" ethnic minorities in their career progression: minority staff are sometimes almost automatically saddled with overseeing D&I efforts. Following the Black Lives Matter protests this summer, many black professionals have attested to being asked to lead diversity projects in their firms, but this is work that they may not be cut out for as individuals, and even if they are interested, they may not be given the resources to make such projects effective or the appropriate support for a task which is, by its nature, challenging to the established

hierarchy. The assumption that they will be "diversity champions" pigeonholes how they are seen. It is still a reality, Hashi Mohamed, barrister and author of People Like Us: What it Takes to Make it in Modern Britain told me, that many BAME employees in elite professions "will be seen as diversity hires, and not future leaders."

Thickening the plot are renewed questions about the very term BAME. Mohamed's story is instructive in this respect. He arrived in Britain as a child refugee from Somalia, grew up in a working-class household, got into Oxford University and now works as a barrister, a singularly hard institution to break into. How much can "BAME," essentially a shorthand for anyone not white, capture the large gulfs of experience between different types of minorities? The official figures suggest that 53 per cent of families with a Bangladeshi head of household are living in poverty, followed by 46 per cent for Pakistani heads; that figure drops to 34 per cent where there is a Chinese head of household, and 24 per cent for Indians, which is still higher than the 19 per cent poverty rate for whites, but far closer to that than it is to the less-prosperous minorities. The term "BAME" looks away from problems that pertain specifically to Britain's black communities. Class differences can also be elided. "Class doesn't crop up enough," Mohamed said, preferring to look at the issue through the lens of both "class and race"—it is not enough for firms to hire middle-class ethnic minorities and announce job done.

***

Perhaps the deepest question concerns how, exactly, obsessing about the make-up of FTSE 100 leadership helps working-class communities who are a long way from the boardroom. Britain's ethnic minority workers are, the Joseph Rowntree Foundation found a few years ago, less likely to receive the living wage compared to white employees. During the pandemic they have been disproportionately required to soldier on in all sorts of essential "front-line" jobs—from hospitals to supermarkets and public transport—and duly suffered disproportionately from illness and death. In this context, some will see basic enforcement and protection as more urgent than aspiration and symbolic breakthroughs.

"Ninety-five per cent of the population will never interact with what's happening at the very top," said Adam Almeida, research analyst at race equality think tank the Runnymede Trust. While it is important to ensure every workplace is discrimination-free, it is also useful to address the limits of what D&I can do. The installation of individuals from ethnic minority backgrounds in positions of power is no guarantee of ushering in inclusive policies, as Britain's recent politics underlines. Boris Johnson has been lauded for the "most ethnically diverse Cabinet ever," but most BAME Britons are probably more interested in how immigration, public health and other policies actually bear on their communities. Refugees reading recent reports that Home Secretary Priti Patel asked "officials to explore the construction of an asylum processing centre on Ascension Island" may not be much interested in her ethnicity. Back in the world of business, a lot hinges on whether organisations that have signed up to the rhetoric of diversity will show willingness to overhaul their own practices: for example, by enrolling BAME casuals and subcontractors as permanent staff.

It is easy for companies to overstate the scope of what they are doing on diversity. Corporate D&I initiatives are, and can only ever be, a limited attempt to support interpersonal relationships and stamp out discrimination in the workplace. It is a worthy goal—but not a proxy for equality writ large.

***

D&I is exactly the sort of discretionary expenditure that gets pared back in a recession. A survey of American D&I leaders this May found that 27 per cent of organisations had put their diversity initiatives on hold due to the pandemic. Meanwhile, new home working practices could aggravate old problems. Agbesanwa of PwC, who also runs a networking group for millennial women in the private sector, said that "speaking up in meetings is hard enough" where race, class or sex is a barrier to confidence, but that Zoom etiquette can also create obstacles—and that working quietly from home can leave effort going unrecognised, particularly by those who aren't used to constant self-promotion. Meanwhile, director of diversity and inclusion at Network Rail, Loraine Martins, explained that with the recent Black Lives Matter protests,

"there's so much attention now… the challenge for us is to make the opportunity sustainable."

The D&I world is filled with necessary doubt and debate—about what works and what doesn't, and whether focusing on the employment practices affecting the elite staff of companies who may be exacerbating social problems elsewhere is anything more than a distraction. There are bad training sessions and good ones, counterproductive ways to talk about race and helpful ones, but at least at my Steps' training seminar, there was nothing "hostile to thought" or any of the hysterical self-denunciations that feature in the right-wing caricatures. What I saw was a group of people discussing how best to support each other's needs.

The effort to think through what we owe one another, and how we best negotiate our differences, is surely one that can only enhance our civic sphere. "I often catch myself being overly cynical about these things and thinking it's just lip service," said Ben, the consultant at the mostly white office, "and I remind myself that the alternative is not even the lip service," describing how harrowing he's found the anti-Muslim violence institutionally normalised in India, his home country. He cited this not in a spirit of indulgent self-congratulation, but instead as reason to keep on keeping on, mindful of what we have gained so far as well as how far we have to go.

Rebecca Liu is assistant editor at Prospect magazine

4 December 2020

What is the circular economy?

A circular economy is part of the solution to our global climate emergency – one in which products, services and systems are designed to maximise their value and minimise waste.

It's an all-encompassing approach to life and business, where everything has value and nothing is wasted. In simple terms, it can be explained as 'make, use, remake' as opposed to 'make, use, dispose'.

Transitioning to a circular economy

The current 'linear' system where everyday products are just made, used and disposed of no longer works for businesses, people or our environment.

The ultimate goal of a circular economy is to design out waste. It's about responsible production where businesses which supply products and services, get the maximum life and value from the natural resources used to make them.

Why do we need a circular economy?

The world's population is expected to peak at 10bn in 2050. Our resources, the earth's raw materials, are not limitless. As a result, global labour and raw material costs are on the increase.

Circular economy business opportunities can offer new ways to mitigate these risks to allow businesses to grow and diversify. In a circular economy, products and materials keep circulating in a high value state of use, through supply chains, for as long as possible.

For this reason, "making things last" is a moral, environmental and economic imperative.

How does a circular economy work?

Businesses, organisations and industries need to embrace the opportunities and benefits of a circular economy so that waste is 'designed out' of how we live - those who can do so first will have a competitive advantage.

A circular economy is achieved by designing products smartly with their whole life cycle in mind, re-using and repairing to extend their useful life, and then when their life is deemed over, remanufacturing to create new products from old.

There are several routes to embracing a circular economy including;

Design

Products are made using regenerative materials and modular design techniques in order to be longer-lasting and easier to disassemble and repair, in essence, to design out waste;

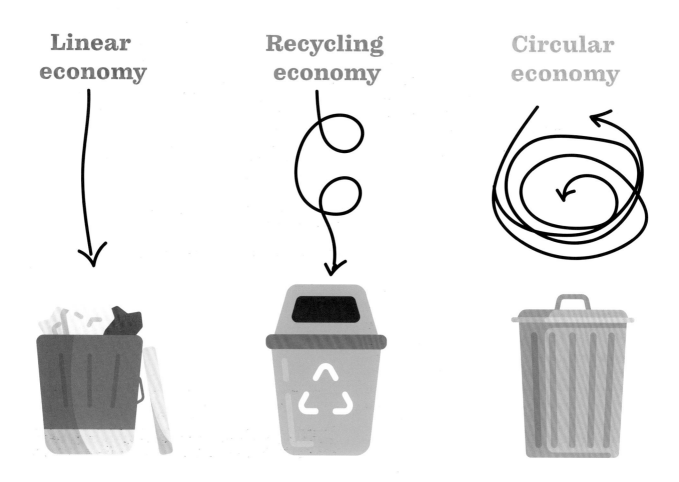

Re-use and repair

Product life cycles are extended by maintenance and repair, so they remain in their original use for as long as possible. This could include manufacturers retaining ownership of their products and implementing re-use and repair services;

Recycling

Products can be easily separated into component parts and materials, enabling use in new products, displacing the use of virgin raw materials;

Manufacturing

Manufacturing products with circular economy principles built in at design;

Remanufacturing and re-use

Extending the lifetime of products at the end of their 'first life' by repurposing them or enabling other, subsequent uses;

Business models including leasing and servistisation;

Overseeing the full lifespan of your products creates a truly stable business model, with a steady income. Every business is different. Moving to a circular business model can sometimes be about making a few small changes that can make a huge difference in the long run.

How will we benefit from a circular economy?

Scotland can show the world another way, pioneering the use of products and resources responsibly.

A circular economy makes business sense and could save Scottish businesses collectively at least £3bn and will contribute to the Scottish Government's aim of sustainable economic growth.

It has the potential to increase productivity and create jobs, whilst reducing carbon emissions and preserving valuable raw materials. In 2015, the Scottish Government launched its first Circular Economy Strategy for Scotland titled "Making Things Last" in which the priorities for moving towards a more circular economy were set out.

The four priority areas identified for action were:

- ◆ Food and drink and the wider bio-economy;
- ◆ Remanufacture;
- ◆ Construction;
- ◆ Energy infrastructure;

A circular economy will benefit Scotland's economy, society and the environment:

- ◆ **Good for the environment:** Reducing our demand for raw materials and maximising the life of products and materials could eradicate up to almost a fifth of Scotland's carbon footprint by 2050;

- ◆ **An opportunity for business:** It makes business sense. By getting the maximum value out of the resources they use, they will gain the competitive benefits of forming longer-lasting relationships with customers, based on the provision of products and services rather than the sale of products alone;

- ◆ **Beneficial to people:** People's quality of life can be improved nationwide through employment opportunities across Scotland. Jobs based on service-models could create jobs, many in higher-paid roles, and are likely to be locally based.

Our global impact

Scotland is leading the way in the circular economy. In 2018, Scotland hosted the Circular Economy Hotspot event in Glasgow. Over 400 business leaders from across the world were inspired by Scotland's innovation and advancement in the circular economy.

1 December 2019

New study deems Amazon worst for 'aggressive' tax avoidance

Transparency campaign Fair Tax Mark says big six tech firms have paid a fraction of tax rate for 10 years.

By Rupert Neate, Wealth correspondent

The big six US tech firms have been accused of "aggressively avoiding" $100bn (£75bn) of global tax over the past decade.

Amazon, Facebook, Google, Netflix, Apple and Microsoft have been named in a report by tax transparency campaign group Fair Tax Mark as avoiding tax by shifting revenue and profits through tax havens or low-tax countries, and for also delaying the payment of taxes they do incur.

The report singles out Amazon, which is run by the world's richest person, Jeff Bezos, as the worst offender. It said the group paid just $3.4bn (£2.6bn) in tax on its income so far this decade despite achieving revenues of $960.5bn and profits of $26.8bn. Fair Tax Mark said this means Amazon's effective tax rate was 12.7% over the decade when the headline tax rate in the US has been 35% for most of that period.

Amazon said the report's "suggestions are wrong" and that the company had "a 24% effective tax rate on profits from 2010-2018". Amazon said the company's "profit margins are low" and that "naturally results in a lower cash tax rate."

Fair Tax Mark said Amazon's accounting was so complicated there was "no way to discern" how much tax Amazon should be paying or is paying in the UK despite its filings to the US tax authorities showing it made $14.5bn in revenue in the UK last year, and $75.8bn over the decade.

Amazon's two UK subsidiaries – Amazon UK Services and Amazon Web Services UK – had combined tax bills of only £83m over the decade, as the bulk of sales are booked via Luxembourg. Amazon UK Services arm paid £14m in corporation tax last year. Paul Monaghan, chief executive of Fair Tax Mark, said: "Our analysis of the long-run effective tax rate of the Silicon Valley Six over the decade to date has found that there is a significant difference between the cash taxes paid and both the headline rate of tax and, more significantly, the reported current tax provisions. We conclude that the corporation tax paid has been much lower than is commonly understood."

Alex Cobham, chief executive of Tax Justice Network, said: "When multinational corporations abuse their tax responsibilities to society, they weaken the supports that our economies need to work well and create wealth.

"By ensuring multinational corporations pay their fair share locally for the wealth created locally by people's work – based on an agreed formula and supplemented by a minimum effective tax rate – governments can strengthen their economies to run smoothly and make a good life possible for everyone."

However, progress towards that goal was damaged last week when 12 small EU countries, including Ireland, blocked

a proposed new rule that would have forced multinationals to reveal how much profit they make and how much tax they pay in each of the 28 member states.

In a statement Amazon said: "Governments write the tax laws and Amazon is doing the very thing they encourage companies to do – paying all taxes due while also investing many billions in creating jobs and infrastructure. Coupled with low margins, this investment will naturally result in a lower cash tax rate."

Facebook, run by Mark Zuckerberg who has a personal fortune of $77bn, has paid just $7.7bn in income taxes this decade, despite making profits of $75.5bn and revenues of $173.1bn, according to the report. The tax paid as a percentage of profit was just 10.2% over the period 2010-18, the lowest of the so-called "Silicon Six".

Facebook said: "We take our tax obligations seriously and pay what we owe in every market we operate. In 2018 we paid $3.8bn in corporation tax globally and our effective tax rate over the last five years is more than 20%. Under current rules we pay the vast majority of the tax we owe in the US as that is where the bulk of our functions, assets and risks are located. Ultimately these are decisions for governments and we support the OECD process which is looking at new international tax rules for the digital economy."

The report also detailed smaller than expected cash tax payments by Google, Netflix, Apple, and Microsoft. All of the companies said they paid the correct amounts of tax and disputed Fair Tax Mark's figures.

2 December 2019

UK by far the biggest enabler of global corporate tax dodging, groundbreaking research finds

Britain has 'single-handedly' done more to undermine world's tax system than any other nation, report finds.

By Ben Chapman

The UK is by far the world's biggest enabler of corporate tax dodging, helping funnel hundreds of billions of dollars away from state coffers, according to an international investigation.

Of the top 10 countries allowing multinationals to avoid paying billions in tax on their profits, four are British overseas territories.

Chancellor Philip Hammond has pledged to crack down on multinationals like Google and Amazon that boost profits by shifting huge sums through low-tax jurisdictions.

But an index published today by the Tax Justice Network found that the UK has "single-handedly" done the most to break down the global corporate tax system which loses an estimated $500bn (£395bn) to avoidance.

The amount dodged globally each year is more than three times the NHS budget or roughly equivalent to the entire Gross Domestic Product (GDP) of Belgium. Tax haven territories linked to Britain are responsible for around a third of the world's corporate tax avoidance risk – more than four times the next greatest contributor, the Netherlands.

Topping the list was the British Virgin Islands, followed by Bermuda and the Cayman Islands – all British overseas territories. Jersey, a Crown dependency, was seventh while the UK itself comes in thirteenth.

Alex Cobham, chief executive at the Tax Justice Network, described the hypocrisy of rich nations which enable tax avoidance as "sickening".

"A handful of the richest countries have waged a world tax war so corrosive, they've broken down the global corporate tax system beyond repair," Mr Cobham said.

"The UK, Netherlands, Switzerland and Luxembourg – the Axis of Avoidance – line their own pockets at the expense of a crucial funding stream for sustainable human progress.

"The ability of governments across the world to tax multinational corporations in order to pay teachers' wages, build hospitals and ensure a level playing field for local businesses has been deliberately and ruthlessly undermined."

The index, which is the first-ever study of its size and scope, scores each country's system based on the degree to which

The UK dominates the most damaging tax havens

Corporate Tax Haven index score of the world's most damaging corporate tax havens in 2019

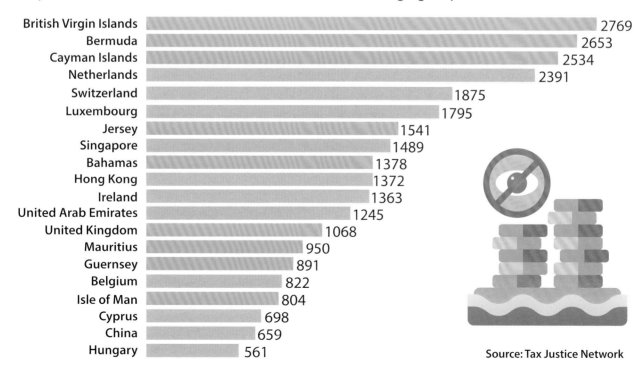

British Virgin Islands	2769
Bermuda	2653
Cayman Islands	2534
Netherlands	2391
Switzerland	1875
Luxembourg	1795
Jersey	1541
Singapore	1489
Bahamas	1378
Hong Kong	1372
Ireland	1363
United Arab Emirates	1245
United Kingdom	1068
Mauritius	950
Guernsey	891
Belgium	822
Isle of Man	804
Cyprus	698
China	659
Hungary	561

Source: Tax Justice Network

The territories marked in light blue are Overseas Territories (OTs) and Crown Dependenceies (CDs) of the UK where the British Queen is head of state. Exceptions are the Bahamas and Mauritius which are British Commonwealth territories but not OTs or CDs

it allows companies to avoid tax. This is then combined with the scale of its corporate activity to determine the share of global taxes put at risk.

It covers 64 jurisdictions and is based on a score reflecting how aggressively they use tax cuts, loopholes, secrecy and other mechanisms to attract multinational activity.

Other countries in the UK network, including Turks and Caicos Islands, Anguilla, the Isle of Man, and Guernsey, also scored highly for allowing corporate tax dodging.

Such countries have prompted a "race to the bottom" that has depleted tax revenues and has particularly harmed poorer nations, the Tax Justice Network said.

While many of the top 10 tax haven territories are tiny, they are home to trillions of dollars of foreign direct investment – suggesting that many of these flows may be motivated by reducing tax bills rather than genuine economic activity.

Labour's shadow chancellor, John McDonnell, said, "The Tories' record on tax avoidance is embarrassing and shameful.

"The only way the UK stands out internationally on tax is in leading a race to the bottom in creating tax loopholes, and dismantling the tax systems of countries in the Global South.

"The rot has to stop. While Tory leadership hopefuls promise tax giveaways for the rich, a Labour government will implement the most comprehensive plan ever seen in the UK to tackle tax avoidance and evasion."

Mr Cobham added: "To curtail the corporate tax avoidance that costs hundreds of billions of dollars every year, governments must finally deliver international rules that ensure profits are declared, and tax paid, in the places where real economic activity takes place.

"Corporations should be taxed where their employees work, not where their ledgers hide."

Christian Aid condemned the UK for "turning a blind eye" to large-scale tax avoidance and contributing to a lack of vital services across the globe.

The charity's global lead on economic justice, Toby Quantrill, said: "The Corporate Tax Haven Index is a critical piece of work that deepens our understanding of just how broken the global economic system really is.

"It highlights the role of the UK and its network of Overseas Territories and Crown Dependencies in undermining the ability of other countries, including some of the poorest in the world, to provide for the most basic rights of their citizens."

He added: "This is a problem that Christian Aid first highlighted more than 10 years ago, and which has been widely acknowledged, yet remains fundamentally unsolved."

A spokesperson for the Treasury said tackling tax avoidance was a priority for the government.

The spokesperson added: "We've been at the forefront of international action to reform global tax rules, using our presidency of the G8 in 2013 to initiate the first substantial renovation of international tax standards in almost a century.

"We also introduced the Diverted Profits Tax to counter aggressive tax planning techniques used by multinationals, and we've secured and protected £200bn in tax revenues since 2010 from compliance activities which would otherwise have gone unpaid."

29 May 2019

Tax havens: there's a chance now to apply conditions to bailouts

THE CONVERSATION

An article from The Conversation.

By Atkul K. Shah, Professor, Accounting and Finance, City, University of London

The huge economic slowdown brought about by COVID-19 has resulted in companies around the world seeking help from their governments. The conditions of these bailouts vary but some countries have notably said that tax avoiders should not benefit. Poland and Denmark were the first, with Austria, France and Italy making similar noises.

Companies that avoid paying tax argue that they operate within the law and do not breach any rules. This may be true. But the outcomes for government purses have been dire. One piece of research found 40% of all corporate tax revenues are parked in tax havens, leading to a tax loss for global society of US$700 billion in 2017 alone.

How can a company that has avoided giving back to the society in which it operates and paying into crucial services now expect to be bailed out?

Good corporate citizenship involves the fair payment of local taxes. For far too long corporations have seen tax as a cost to their business rather than a repayment to the stakeholders that provide key infrastructure and services like roads, police and hospitals.

At the same time, there has been rising global competition between states to attract foreign business investment. This results in a race to the bottom for countries trying to raise tax revenues, with offshore tax havens often charging zero taxes for the businesses based there.

Over the last few decades, giant multinationals have got away with very little in the way of corporate tax payments. Exposés like the Luxembourg leaks revealed how companies shift their profits from the country where they were earned (such as the UK) to a country that has a much lower corporate tax rate (such as Luxembourg). These are the same tax receipts that pay for the hospitals struggling to cope with the surge in demand from COVID-19 sufferers.

There is an entire industry set up around this practice. Armies of lawyers, bankers and accountants enable companies to funnel their profits to low-tax jurisdictions. This may be legal but instead of helping states protect their infrastructures and services, this erodes their tax receipts.

Open to debate is the definition of a tax haven. The EU has its official list of "noncooperative jurisdictions for tax purposes". This includes places like the Cayman Islands and Panama, which are outside of the EU. Yet some of the biggest tax havens are in the EU, including Luxembourg and Ireland.

This is a highly sensitive and political issue. But the reality is that it has become normal for multinationals to even shift their profits from one EU country to other EU countries which have lower corporate tax rates. One study finds that France, for example, loses 22% of its corporate revenue to tax havens – 18% of this goes to other EU countries. In 2017 it lost US$13 billion, of which more than US$11 billion went mostly to Luxembourg, Belgium, the Netherlands and Ireland.

Another recent study by the Tax Justice Network think tank found that Italy and Spain – both badly hit by coronavirus – lost significant tax revenues (US$1.5 billion and US$1 billion, respectively) to the Netherlands in 2017. Yet most of the recent announcements by countries to not give state aid to tax avoiders only use the EU's official list.

A long-term solution

A better solution to this problem would be to introduce country-by-country reporting. This would allow investors and government to accurately tell where a company trades, where it parks its profits, and where and what taxes it actually pays. Considering accounting has international standards and most big corporations are audited by one of the Big Four auditing firms, this should be relatively easy to implement.

Unfortunately, however, researchers have shown time and again – for example in the creation of privatised international accounting standards or the dominance of the Big Four global accounting firms – how the practice of accounting is highly political and captured by powerful corporate interests. As a result, more and more of the tax burden falls on ordinary people who have less power and influence over their tax affairs.

Now that we are in a profound economic crisis, with a number of multinationals reliant on state aid, we have a unique opportunity to change business as usual. Corporations are in trouble and seeking state aid so governments can now call the shots, and make sure that money is not given away without conditions. Such conditions can include not having a subsidiary in a tax haven, transparency about profits earned in each country, and greater openness and commitment to paying fair taxes in the countries where revenues are earned.

This will require genuine global cooperation on tax matters. A race to the bottom between countries for tax collection should no longer be tolerated. At stake are the jobs, pensions, education and healthcare for citizens in every country.

29 April 2020

Key Facts

- Data shows that online shopping in 2016 involved 1.66 billion digital buyers around the world – this has been forecast to grow to 2.14 billion by 2021. (page 2)

- Half (52%) of UK businesses view COVID-19 as the greater barrier to business over leaving the Brexit transition period without a trade deal. (page 6)

- 9 in 10 Captains of Industry agree the impact of COVID-19 is one of the most important issues facing Britain today. (page 7)

- A third (of Britain's business elite) see no opportunities for their company in relation to Brexit. (page 7)

- As result of Covid 19 and Brexit, more than 250,000 small firms expect to fold in 2021 without further government financial support, according to a quarterly poll by the Federation of Small Businesses. (page 11)

- According to Yahoo Finance, the global crowdfunding market is set to grow at a rate of 16 per cent over the next five years. (page 14)

- Recent research shows over a third of 18 to 34 year olds want to launch an independent enterprise in 2021, compared to 28% of 35 to 54 year olds. (page 22)

- More than 400,000 people formed a company in 2019, and the UK is on track to reach the milestone of over half a million people starting a business within the space of a year for the sixth year running. (page 23)

- Recent surveys show that more than 60% of young people say they want to be their own boss. (page 23)

- Soon after the EU referendum, a KPMG survey showed that 76% of the 1,300 CEOs surveyed around the world were looking to relocate the headquarters of their firms. (page 25)

- According to a World Value Index survey, only 14 percent of employees say their values are well-aligned with the companies for which they work. Nearly a third think that corporations only support specific to causes to makes themselves look good or accrue tax benefits. (page 26)

- Research from Sodexo Engageshows that 87% of employees believe that the success of a business should be measured in terms of more than just its financial performance and 64% would not take a job if a potential employer did not take CSR seriously. (page 26)

- There are now more than 2,900 certified B Corps in more than 60 countries, cutting across industries and sectors. (page 27)

- In 2017, an independent government-backed report (Parker Review) discovered that over 50 per cent of FTSE 100 companies had no ethnic minority directors. Black, Asian and minority ethnic (BAME) board members made up just 8 per cent of the UK's total, while the UK BAME population is 14 per cent. (page 29)

- The world's population is expected to peak at 10bn in 2050. (page 34)

- Of the top 10 countries allowing multinationals to avoid paying billions in tax on their profits, four are British overseas territories. (page 37)

- The amount of tax dodged globally each year is more than three times the NHS budget or roughly equivalent to the entire Gross Domestic Product (GDP) of Belgium. (page 37)

- One piece of research found 40% of all corporate tax revenues are parked in tax havens, leading to a tax loss for global society of US$700 billion in 2017 alone. (page 38)

B-Corps

Certified B Corporations, also known as B-Corps are businesses that meet the highest standards of social and environmental performance, balancing profit and purpose.

Capitalism

An economic system in which wealth generation is driven by privately-owned enterprises and individuals, rather than the state.

Circular economy

Keeping resources for as long as possible in order to extract maximum value from them, and then reusing or recycling the product (or materials from the product) instead of throwing it away.

Competition law

A law that regulates 'anti-competitive' conduct by companies.

Corporate social responsibility (CSR)

Corporate social responsibility, or CSR, is a concept closely linked to business ethics. It refers to self-regulation by a business or corporation, which is built into their overall business model. Companies which are serious about CSR will conduct their business in an ethical way and in the interests of the wider community (and society at large).

Crowdsourcing/crowdfunding

Funding a project, business or venture by raising multiple small amounts of money from the public. This is usually done via the Internet, and usually offers contributors something in exchange for their donation, e.g. those who donate towards publication of a book, may receive a signed copy and other merchandise.

Ecommerce

Ecommerce, or electronic commerce, refers to transactions conducted via the internet.

Entrepreneur

An individual who starts and runs their own business.

Freelancer

People who work for themselves and contract out their services.

Gross Domestic Product (GDP)

The total value of the goods and services produced in a country within a year. This figure is used as a measure of a country's economic performance.

Investment

Investing money into a venture or project in return for profit.

National living wage

The national living wage is now £9.15 an hour for those living in London and £7.85 in the rest of the UK. This is the amount that the Government believes is the minimum people need to be paid in order to achieve a basic standard of living in which all necessities can be paid for.

Private sector

Businesses/economy that is not under state control.

Service industry

A business that provides goods but does not manufacture them, for example catering.

Shadow economy

Illicit economic activity.

Shareholder

Anyone who owns shares in a company or corporation.

SMEs

This stands for small and medium-sized enterprises. It describes any company with fewer than 250 employees.

Tax avoidance

Corporations or individuals exploit legal loopholes to pay as little tax as they can.

Tax evasion

Fraudulent action to avoid paying taxes by individuals or businesses. Tax evasion is a crime.

Turnover

The total amount of business done in a given time.

Activities

Brainstorming

♦ In small groups, discuss what you know about business in the UK.

  • What different types of businesses are there?

  • Why do some people choose to become entrepreneurs?

  • What is business education like in your school?

  • What does D&I (Diversity & Inclusion) mean in business terms?

  • Which types of businesses have been affected positively and which type have been affected negatively by the Covid-19 pandemic? Give some examples.

Research

♦ Conduct a survey to find out how many students in your school would consider becoming entrepreneurs and starting their own business when they leave school, instead of going to college or university. Write a report that summarises your findings and include graphs to illustrate your results.

♦ Do some research to find out about a famous entrepreneur then create a presentation to share your research with your class.

♦ Imagine that you have been given £500 to start a business. What would you do? In small groups, plan how you would invest your £500 and then share with the rest of your class. You should carefully consider your start-up costs and expected profits.

♦ Research a global brand such as Sony and investigate how many countries they sell their products in and where they have offices/factories. Share your findings with a classmate.

Design

♦ Choose an article from this book and create an illustration to highlight its key themes.

♦ Design a scheme that could run within your school to encourage entrepreneurial activity among students. Write a summary of your scheme and how it will work.

♦ Read the article on page 23: *Five young entrepreneurs from Scotland win national award*. Choose one of the winning innovations and create a logo for it.

♦ Imagine that you work for a website that allows people to 'crowdsource' their business ideas. Create a series of web banners and draft a marketing e-mail that you could distribute to raise awareness of your platform.

Oral

♦ "Universities are the best place to start a business." Discuss this statements in small groups.

♦ Imagine that you work for your family business but you think you could make improvements to run the business in a more socially and environmentally responsible way. What would you say to your family members to convince them to apply for B-Corps certification? Role play the situation.

♦ How important is corporate responsibility to you when you choose brands/products? Do you actively boycott certain companies? Write a list of companies you believe strike a balance between profit and purpose and whose values align with your own, and a list of companies you avoid. Compare notes with a partner and discuss your choices.

♦ What is 'competition law' and do you think it is fair? Discuss in small groups.

♦ In groups, stage your own version of the television programme The Apprentice.

♦ Is there a moral duty to pay taxes? What is the difference between tax avoidance and tax evasion? Discuss as a class.

Reading/writing

♦ Write a one-paragraph definition of globalisation.

♦ Imagine that you have decided to start your own business. Write a blog post exploring the motivation behind your decision.

♦ Choose one of the illustrations from this book and write 300 words exploring what you think the artist was trying to portray with their image.

♦ Make a list of the benefits and risks associated with becoming an entrepreneur. Would you ever consider starting your own business?

♦ Write a letter to your headteacher, explaining why you think it is important for students to have 'real world' business experience.

Index

Acknowledgements

The publisher is grateful for permission to reproduce the material in this book. While every care has been taken to trace and acknowledge copyright, the publisher tenders its apology for any accidental infringement or where copyright has proved untraceable. The publisher would be pleased to come to a suitable arrangement in any such case with the rightful owner.

The material reproduced in ISSUES books is provided as an educational resource only. The views, opinions and information contained within reprinted material in ISSUES books do not necessarily represent those of Independence Educational Publishers and its employees.

Images

Cover image courtesy of iStock. All other images courtesy of Pixabay and Unsplash.

Icons

Icons on page 34 were made by Freepik and smashicons, www.flaticon.com.

Illustrations

Simon Kneebone: pages 13, 17 & 31.

Angelo Madrid: pages 1, 14 & 22.

Additional acknowledgements

With thanks to the Independence team: Shelley Baldry, Danielle Lobban, Jackie Staines and Jan Sunderland.

Tracy Biram

Cambridge, January 2021